Supervision and Treatment Experiences of Probationers with Mental Illness

Emerging from a qualitative research study on the rehabilitation experiences of adult male probationers with mental health illness, this book describes the treatment and rehabilitation experiences of these individuals and contextualizes their experiences within the landscape of mental health treatment in the United States. Often underserved in outpatient community support programs, probationers with mental health illness (PMIs) face stigma and obstacles in seeking mental health treatment and rehabilitation. Examining the lived experiences of both PMIs and their probation officers, this book offers insights into the study of stigma as it relates to probationers and the work of probation officers in furthering treatment and rehabilitation options for PMIs.

Babatunde Oluwaseun Adekson, PhD, is a writer and researcher at Virginia Polytechnic Institute and State University, USA.

Supervision and Treatment Experiences of Probationers with Mental Illness

Analyses of Contemporary Issues in Community Corrections

Babatunde Oluwaseun Adekson, PhD

Routledge
Taylor & Francis Group

NEW YORK AND LONDON

First published 2019
by Routledge
711 Third Avenue, New York, NY 10017

and by Routledge
2 Park Square, Milton Park, Abingdon, Oxon, OX14 4RN

Routledge is an imprint of the Taylor & Francis Group, an informa business

© 2019 Taylor & Francis

British Library Cataloguing-in-Publication Data
A catalogue record for this book is available from the British Library

Library of Congress Cataloguing-in-Publication Data
A catalog record has been requested for this book

ISBN: 978-1-138-74683-1 (hbk)
ISBN: 978-1-315-18041-0 (ebk)

Typeset in Times New Roman
by Deanta Global Publishing Services, Chennai, India

Contents

Figures

1 Introduction
Summary of this Investigation

The number of individuals legally committed to community corrections and probation sentences has increased dramatically in recent years (Ditton, 1999; Glaze & Bonzcar, 2007). This growing population of offenders experiences challenges in multiple domains of life, including rehabilitation/recidivism, housing, employment, education, and access to therapeutically effective and culturally relevant mental health care (Skeem, Emke-Francis, & Louden, 2006). Skeem et al. (2006) argued that individuals with mental illness who are forced into the criminal justice system are a particularly vulnerable group. This vulnerability is related to the fact that they simultaneously experience barriers and challenges related to their criminal history, the stigma of deviance, and the stigma of mental illness (Falk, 2001).

More than 50 years ago, Goffman (1963) defined "stigma" as any label that conveys a discrediting influence on the target individual or population. This term is particularly germane to this study of Probationers with Mental Illness (PMIs) in that they are often marginalized as a result of their prior criminal activity and psychosocial integration challenges. Moreover, the institutional and structural make-up of probation—coupled with the potential for stigma to impact and/or overshadow the experience of PMIs and their mandated interactions with their Probation Officers (POs)—present formidable barriers to effective post-incarceration services. To elucidate the influence of stigma, commonly constructed public perceptions about mental illness and deviant behaviors are described, along with the influences of these social constructions to the processes of stigma maintenance. By focusing on the experiences of PMIs relative to the potential of stigma-laden processes in probation work—coupled with the views of the POs assigned to assist them—this qualitative investigation is expected to fill a gap in the existing literature.

Overview of the Problem

In comparison to the "average" probationer, probationers with mental illness are likely to experience the criminal justice system and subsequent rehabilitation services quite differently due to their special needs and challenges (Allen, 1985). However, a thorough understanding of the experiences of PMIs with agencies targeted to help them has yet to be achieved. This lack of attention to the experiences of probationers has, in fact, limited the success of rehabilitation programs and leads to the perception that former inmates released into the community are "less than complete human beings, unworthy, and less deserving than citizens who have not violated the law" (Allen, 1985, p. 67). In support of the need to provide a voice for probationers, Chui (2003) asserted that if the field of probation and the larger criminal justice system is to make a comprehensive ideological transition toward addressing the types of identified deficits, probationers must be allowed to describe their opinions as service consumers.

Probation work in the American criminal justice system has evolved in the last century and a half. The structure and process of probation as a service have also grown from strictly law enforcement to include rehabilitation and care. In addition, the nature of probation work, the types of skills and expertise that POs have—coupled with the dispositions and attitudes they employ in their work—necessitates the use of client-centered techniques to aid in the "assessment, planning, interventions and evaluation" (Durnsecu, 2011, p. 194) of PMIs' mental health and rehabilitative needs. PMIs have specific service needs, which are too often constrained in the structure of probation, rehabilitation, and treatment experiences. Specifically, their probationary experiences are shaped by the nature of their mental health issue(s), their treatment protocols, their relationship with their POs, and the potentially pernicious influence of stigmatization on rehabilitation services. All these issues impact how they utilize probation as a service.

Significance of the Problem

Probationers with Mental Illness

According to a 2006 Bureau of Justice Statistics report, 64% of incarcerated individuals will present with a recent mental health issue (Steadman, Osher, Robbins, Case, & Samuels, 2009). This finding supports earlier research that a disproportionately large number of people with a mental illness (diagnosed or undiagnosed) are arrested in comparison to the general population (Lamb & Weinberger, 1998); moreover, approximately 6% to 15% of individuals in city and county criminal justice institutions and 10% to 15% of individuals in state institutions are dealing with *severe* mental illness. Important for this investigation is that from 6% to 9% of the nation's probationers present with a serious mental illness (Lurigio & Swartz, 2000).

In addition to meeting standard conditions of probation (i.e., maintaining employment and meeting requirements for medication compliance), the PMI is typically required to participate in mental health treatment as a special condition of probation—often in complex and overburdened mental health care and rehabilitation systems (Louden, Skeem, Camp, & Christensen, 2008; Skeem et al., 2006). Indeed, the literature shows that only 15% of the probation departments that responded to a national survey indicated that they operated targeted programs for PMIs (Lurigio & Swartz, 2000). Moreover, PMIs who present with less outwardly expressed symptoms of mental illness usually receive scant attention from probation officers, particularly in traditional probation rehabilitation models. Compounding the problem is that the vast majority of probation officers generally lack the experience and background necessary to deal effectively with emotionally troubled clients.

In short, PMIs are an underserved population, and most traditional-model probation officers are unable to adequately handle the complexities of care that these individuals need (Lurigio & Swartz, 2000). Thus, much more needs to be done to improve the programmatic delivery process, particularly in terms of communicating expectations in more humane ways (i.e., positive attitudinal, relational, and professional competencies) for these individuals.

Stigma

Stigma has long been linked to those dealing with mental illness. The term "stigma" is a mark of disgrace meant to discredit the targeted individual (Byrne, 2000; Goffman, 1963). Modern conceptualizations of stigma emphasize the connections between labeling, stereotyped attributions, emotional or prejudicial reactions (i.e., attitudes), and various types of discrimination (Arboleda-Florez & Stuart, 2012). "Unpredictable," "dangerous," and "violent" are just some of the types of characterizations and labels that individuals with severe mental illness are given in the larger cultural milieu—and this type of labeling is increasing as a result of killing events that seem to occur far too frequently (e.g., Roseburg, Sandy Hook, Virginia Tech, Columbine, etc.).

Additionally, there is the potential for individuals with relatively less-stigmatized mental illnesses to self-stigmatize based on the commonly accepted misconceptions and societal beliefs about mental illness in our culture (Corrigan & Kleinlein, 2005). In addition to the particular relationship processes mentioned above, the role of stigma in the relationship between service professionals and their clientele with mental health issues is an important consideration. As such, one must consider the kinds of relational practices of POs and contextualized ideologies and structural arrangements within the probation systems that PMIs could potentially perceive as stigmatizing. These considerations are important both in terms of the mental health status of PMIs as well as the likelihood of them staying out of jails and prison. In short, mental illness stigma can take several forms (self, public, and structural) and is known to be debilitating for those who experience it.

In addition to mental illness stigma, Falk (2001) pointed out that individuals who are convicted of a crime also possess a stigma (i.e., the stigma of criminality, deviance, or stigma of conviction) that labels them long after incarceration—and, depending on the crime, perhaps forever. There are inherent challenges associated with this devalued identity in that these individuals often find it difficult to assimilate back into mainstream society due to employment hindrances and other social impediments. They also experience a change in status and therefore seek the company of others with similar devalued identities; thus, in some instances they transform their stigma into a status symbol within their circle of "criminals." In essence, the stigma of criminality or deviance does not normally culminate when a probationer has finished his or her prison sentence or probationary period. Those who have been impacted by the "criminal" or "convict" label continue to be perceived with a good deal of suspicion.

The problem, therefore, is that PMIs are at risk for the "double-stigma" of being labeled a criminal-deviant and also possessing the label of being mentally ill (Corrigan & Kleinlein, 2005). In addition, the institutional mandates that are built into the probation system could be potentially structurally stigmatizing. Once a person gets involved in the criminal justice system, he or she enters "a parallel universe in which discrimination, stigma, and exclusion are perfectly legal ... It does not matter whether [the criminally deviant] actually spent time in prison; [his or her] second-class citizenship begins the moment [he or she is arrested and charged with a crime]" (Alexander, 2012, p. 94).

Purpose of the Study

This qualitative study was designed to investigate the treatment and rehabilitation experiences of PMIs, who are often underserved in outpatient and community support programs (Arboleda-Florez & Stuart, 2012; Byrne, 2000; Shoham & Rahav, 1982). To ensure a comprehensive understanding of this issue, I also examined the experiential context and perspectives of the service professionals/probation officers who were tasked with helping the PMIs fully transition back into the community after their release. This dual lens facilitated an examination of how PMIs self-report about the "what" and "how" aspects of their probation sentence, while the POs' perspectives offered a look into how treatment and rehabilitation practices (i.e., structural and institutional ideologies of probation work) are conceptualized and implemented. A third aim was to understand the role of stigma in the practice of probation. This study was designed to fill a scholarly gap by conceptualizing the discourses that probationers use to describe their experience(s) in the mental health and criminal justice systems.

Research Question

To guide this investigation, the researcher developed the following overarching research question: *How do PMIs experience probation with a particular probation officer?* This question was prompted by the need to explore the probationary experiences of PMIs and how they perceive the impact of the practices of POs and the resultant structure and expectations of POs, as well as the institutional ideologies of the probation process on PMIs' treatment and rehabilitation experiences.

Significance of the Study

By expanding our understanding of the lived experiences of PMIs as they transition back into society—with a particular emphasis on how the discourses, perceptions, and practices of their PO impacted and shaped the experience of the PMI (Marshall & Rossman, 2011)—this study is expected to add to the literature by offering some conceptual insights into the study of stigma as it relates to the experience of PMIs and the work of service professionals in three areas: knowledge, public policy, and treatment options for practitioners.

Contribution to Knowledge

The findings from this study may increase our understanding of (1) the debilitating and pervasive influence of mental illness in our nation's probationer population, (2) the structural limitations in society that are likely to hinder their progress toward wellness and their ability to re-enter society as contributing members, and (3) the crippling role that stigma plays in their lives. Indeed, this study suggests that stigma plays a major role in thwarting their ability to overcome both their stamp as a former prisoner—but even more so as a person with a diagnosed mental illness in need of empathy and understanding instead of vilification.

Relevance to Public Policy

Although researchers, policy makers, and clinicians are aware of the high prevalence of mental disorders among incarcerated individuals, there is little empirical work to assess the burden of such conditions on probationers—despite the fact that probation is the most commonly used disposition in the criminal justice system (Crilly, Caine, Lamberti, Brown, & Friedman, 2009). And as noted earlier, available post-incarceration justice programs tend to be deficient in terms of their services for PMIs. Also germane to any discussion of policy changes for probationers with mental illness is that they are typically at higher risk for substance abuse disorders (drugs and alcohol), homelessness, non/under-employment, and physical abuse (Ditton, 1999). Thus, findings from this study may add to a growing discourse on the structural policy changes that will benefit this vulnerable population.

Usefulness to Practitioners

Although one can argue that the United States has made extraordinary advances in treating those with mental illness, most mental health disorders—similar to chronic physical disorders—require ongoing treatment. The difference with mental illness, however, is that treatment protocols typically involve a multi-pronged approach that could include medication, one-on-one psychotherapy, and group therapy. What makes the treatment of PMIs additionally complex is the added level of probationary requirements that require the input of a PO. Psychiatrists are not the only health-care practitioners who are skilled in treating mental illness; other qualified personnel include mental health counselors, social workers, pastoral counselors, clinical psychologists—and probation officers in the case of this study's cohort. It is hoped that findings from this investigation will advance the training protocols of POs and others involved in the care of PMIs so that these PMIs don't end up in a revolving door of incarceration.

Overview of Methodology

This qualitative inquiry was designed to give voice to probationers with mental illness—individuals amongst the most marginalized and stigmatized groups in contemporary American society. Specifically, the project provided PMIs with the opportunity to relate their probationary experiences, and to provide insight into how these experiences were shaped by the practices of their POs. This investigation was designed and implemented around the experiences of PMIs within a county probation system. To address the research question, one-on-one semi-structured interviews were conducted with six PMIs (Appendix A) and six POs (Appendix B), which were supplemented by participant observations of PMI–PO interactions.

The "self" as a researcher is an especially important consideration in qualitative research, as it speaks to the issue of reflexivity, which involves examining one's conceptual preconceptions and motivations. In other words, due to the salient influence of the "self" of the researcher, it became important for me to be aware of, and consistently self-reflect about my roles and motivations in the methodological decisions. This goal was facilitated through the use of journals and analytic memos throughout the data collection and analysis processes. Grounded theory was used as the analytical lens through which codes and data were subsequently scrutinized. This process entailed collecting information about the actions and interactions inherent in this probation context, reflecting on their meanings, making tentative interpretations about the data, arriving at and evaluating conclusions, and eventually discussing outcomes of this study in terms of related processes and concepts (Marshall & Rossman, 2011). In short, in conducting this research, I engaged in a "process of trying to gain a better understanding of the complexities of human experience" (Marshall & Rossman, 2011, p. 55) in this particular probation context.

Theoretical Framework

The theoretical presuppositions about stigma as they relate to marginalized groups (i.e., incarcerated and community-sentenced criminal offenders and individuals with mental illness) have played a major role in informing the focus of this investigation. Specifically, the deleterious impact of institutionalization—coupled with intra-culturally sanctioned stigma—are likely to alter the help-seeking tendencies for a large cohort of marginalized individuals, thereby impacting the wellness paradigm for a growing cohort of individuals with mental illness. The challenges of the stigmatized experience are typically compounded by probationers' reduced socioeconomic status and limited educational attainment, which also compromises the ability of those with mental illness to access consistent, high-quality mental health services.

There are particular applications of the historical beliefs and practices regarding stigma and contemporary stigma-formation processes relative to individuals labeled as deviants or undesirables. There are also relevant theories of stigma formation that will be explicated that have empirical foundations in psychology and sociology. These include labeling theory, a socio-cognitive model of self-stigma, motivational models, and authoritarian and social dominance models. All of these models provide distinct perspectives into the ways that stigma is created and perpetuated both intra-personally and interpersonally.

Stigma could potentially impact the experience of those in the criminal justice system throughout the course of their post-incarceration rehabilitation experiences and this will be explored in this study. The power-based and hierarchical relationships between the offender and the criminal-justice professional is inherently stigmatizing, particularly within certain contexts where the ideology of the system mandates the use of coercive processes to force the offender to comply. Stigma is made worse for the offender with a diagnosable mental health condition in that they experience a double—and in some cases triple—level of stigma with respect to mental illness, deviance, and their criminal history.

In addition, to the use of stigma theory, the findings in this study will be interpreted using two developmental theories: Theory of Cognitive Transformation and Theory of Psychosocial Development. Both theories have excellent utility from a human development and a developmental-psychology perspective. They both provide a means for understanding the particular developmental challenges and processes that have either constrained or facilitated individual PMIs' movement through distinct life cycles and stages. Both theories are efficacious in describing and interpreting the cognitive shifts that PMIs experienced by virtue of the probation process. Moreover, examining the narratives that PMIs used to describe their daily navigations of the mandates of probation and of their interactions with their individual POs through the lens of these theories contextualizes PMI's experiences with a developmental framework that may demystify their histories.

Definition of Terms

Mental Illness: Mental illness is defined in the diagnostic and statistical manual (DSM-5) of mental disorders as a behavioral or psychological pattern in an individual that is a result of an underlying psychobiological issue or dysfunction. In addition, these patterns are impactful enough that they create significant distress or impairments in varied areas of functioning (i.e., social, occupational, and educational). These patterns are not merely the commonly accepted reactions to stressors and are not resultant from social deviance in the larger milieu (APA, 2013).

Probationary Officers (POs): A Probation Officer is a "public official authorized to accomplish presentence reports and supervise probationers" (Abadinsky, 2012, p. 338).

Probationers with Mental Illness (PMIs): Typically refers to offenders, with diagnosed mental health problems, whose sentences are diverted to community-based probation settings (Louden et al., 2008).

Rehabilitation: refers to the intensive supervision-based interventions that probationers are expected to adhere to as a component of their probation sentences. The aim of rehabilitation is that increased probationer contact maximizes rehabilitation while allowing for greater offender control. Contemporary rehabilitation programs are usually designed to ease the burden of prison overcrowding (Abadinsky, 2012).

Stigma: refers to a mark of disgrace that is meant to identify an individual's deviance regarding a particular life circumstance, quality, or behavior (Oxford University Press, 2015).

My Positionality

Throughout both my master's program in community mental health counseling and in my doctoral training in counselor education, I expanded on my knowledge of the criminal justice system and, in particular, how the stigma of mental illness has impacted outcomes for PMIs. Specifically, I came to this investigation with a significant level of prior *in vivo* experiences with both probation officers and PMIs.

During my master's training, I completed a clinical internship in a county jail working as a counseling intern with inmate-clients in a mental health and chemical dependency counseling program. While this experience afforded me the opportunity to observe the specific challenges that criminal offenders face, it also enabled me to give voice to these individuals using counseling interventions and advocacy. In addition to my work in the county jail, I have also worked as a therapist in a private practice with federal probationers convicted of drug-related and/or violent offenses. Coupled with my master's-related training, this experience exposed me to the complex and multi-level challenges that federal probationers face in terms of navigating the probation system, finding employment, engaging in rehabilitation and treatment, and living a crime-free lifestyle. I have also worked with adjudicated and county probationers in a mentoring and employment training capacity at a nonprofit agency.

In the summer of 2013, I completed a comprehensive program evaluation of a local county probation system that focused on the ideology and efficacy of their practices and processes. For the evaluation, I interviewed the Commissioner of Probation and was privileged to receive an insider's perspective into how probation plays a role in the criminal justice process. For example, I discovered that the mission of the agency is to maintain public safety first and foremost, which is accomplished through assessing, investigating, and supervising offenders via counseling and referrals to varied community treatment and rehabilitation programs.

My positionality was also informed by my lived experiences as a Nigerian-American man who relocated back to the United States at the age of 12, which alludes to my interest in the role of stigma in that my personal experiences with a series of cultural disconnections impacted my life as a student and citizen in multiple dimensions of life. Specifically, my experiences as a Black male with respect to stereotyping, discrimination, and prejudice in racially charged institutions and in society have heightened my interest in this area and reinforced the importance of giving voice to those impacted by stigma. Based on my personal and academic history and experiences in the criminal justice system, I am well-positioned as a student-researcher, writer, and social advocate to undertake this investigation of the processes of stigma formation within a selected cohort of probationers with mental illness.

Assumptions and Limitations

An overarching assumption driving this investigation is that individuals with mental illness are negatively impacted by societal labeling/stigma and by the debilitating nature of the disease. A related assumption is that PMIs are doubly impacted by the added stigma of their criminal history. (One could argue for a "triple threat" if their self-stigmatization is added to the picture.) The validity of the findings presented herein is predicated on the belief that the PMIs and POs responded honestly to the interview protocols.

This study features several limitations. As with any qualitative study—and especially one targeting a sensitive topic—respondents may not have felt free or safe to voice their true perceptions, despite assurances of anonymity. This study was also limited to a small cohort of male respondents from one county probation system with certain categories of mental illness; this lack of diversity limits its generalizability to a wider population of PMIs. Similarly, the views of the POs who took part in this study cannot be considered to be representative of all the men and women who engage with probationers with mental illness. There were also limitations in the processes used to select the PMI-subjects.

Selection bias is a potentially difficult and challenging issue to resolve, and identifying and choosing PMIs who fit certain study criteria represents an inherently limiting factor in this study. Conversely, it is possible that having a larger subject selection process could have expanded this study's findings by including the experiences and options of a broader cohort of participants.

Chapter Summary and Overview

This chapter provided the rationale for this qualitative study examining the experiences of probationers with mental illness. In particular, this introductory chapter focused on the significance of the problem, the expected contributions of this investigation to the growing scholarship on mental illness, as well as to those trained to help this population, and the varied definitions and conceptualizations of stigma.

Chapter 2 focuses on the methodology and a summary of the qualitative methods that were used to conceptualize this investigation, identify participants, gather data, and analyze findings. Chapters 3 and 4 provide a summary of results and findings from the semi-structured interviews with PMIs and POs, buttressed by the data garnered from the shadowing and observations of the PMI–PO dyad. Chapter 5 includes a discussion of findings, the implications of this investigation, its limitations, and recommendations for future research.

References

Abadinsky, H. (2012). *Probation and parole: Theory and practice.* Upper Saddle River, NJ: Pearson Education, Inc.

Alexander, M. (2012). *The new Jim Crow: Mass incarceration in the age of colorblindness.* New York: The New Press.

Allen, G. F. (1985). The probationers speak: Analysis of the probationers' experiences and attitudes. *Federal Probation,* 49, 67–75.

American Psychiatric Association (APA) (2013). *Diagnostic and statistical manual of mental disorders,* fifth edition. Arlington, VA: American Psychiatric Publishing.

Arboleda-Florez, J., & Stuart, H. (2012). From sin to science: Fighting the stigmatization of mental illness. *Canadian Journal of Psychiatry,* 57(8), 457–463.

Byrne, P. (2000). Stigma of mental illness and ways of diminishing it. *Advances in Psychiatric Treatment,* 6, 65–72.

Chui, W. H. (2003). Experiences of probation supervision in Hong Kong: Listening to the young adult probationers. *Journal of Criminal Justice,* 31, 567–577.

Corrigan, P. W., & Kleinlein, P. (2005). The impact of mental illness stigma. In P. W. Corrigan (Ed), *On the stigma of mental illness: Practical strategies for research and social change* (pp. 11–44). Washington, DC: American Psychological Association.

Crilly, J. F., Caine, E. D., Lamberti, J. S., Brown, T., & Friedman, B. (2009). Mental health services use and symptom prevalence in a cohort of adults on probation. *Psychiatric Services,* 60(4), 542–544.

Ditton, P. M. (1999). *Mental health and treatment of inmates and probationers.* U.S. Department of Justice Special Report. Pub no NCJ-174463. Washington, DC: Department of Justice.

Durnsecu, I. (2011). What matters most in probation supervision: Staff characteristics, staff skills or programme? *Criminology and Criminal Justice.* 12(2), 193–216.

Falk, G. (2001). *Stigma: How we treat outsiders.* Amherst, NY: Prometheus Books.

Glaze, L. E., & Bonczar, T. P. (2007). *Probation and parole in the United States, 2006.* Department of Justice Report. Pub no NCJ-220218. Washington, DC: Department of Justice.

Goffman, E. (1963). *Stigma: Notes on the management of spoiled identity.* New York, NY: Simon & Schuster, Inc.

Lamb, H. R., & Weinberger, L. E. (1998). Persons with severe mental illness in jails and prisons: A review. *Psychiatric Services,* 49(4), 483–492.

Louden, J. E., Skeem, J. L., Camp, J., & Christensen, E. (2008). Supervising probationers with mental disorder: How do agencies respond to violations? *Criminal Justice Behavior,* 35, 832–847.

Lurigio, A. J., & Swartz, J. A. (2000). Changing the contours of the criminal justice system to meet the needs of persons with serious mental illness. *Criminal Justice,* 3, 45–108.

Marshall, C., & Rossman, G. (2011). *Designing qualitative research,* Fifth Edition. London: Sage.

Oxford University Press (2015, November 4). "Stigma." Oxford Dictionary. Retrieved from http://www.oxforddictionaries.com/us/definition/american_english/stigma

Shoham, S. G., & Rahav, G. (1982). *The Mark of Cain: The stigma theory of crime and social deviance*. New York, NY: St. Martin's Press.

Skeem, J. L., Emke-Francis, P., & Louden, J. E. (2006). Probation, mental health, and mandated treatment: A national survey. *Criminal Justice and Behavior*, 33, 158–184.

Steadman, H. J., Osher, F. C., Robbins, P. C., Case, B., & Samuels, S. (2009). Prevalence of serious mental illness among jail inmates. *Psychiatric Services*, 60(6), 761–765.

2 Methodology

This study was designed to answer the following research question: *How do PMIs experience probation with a particular probation officer?* This chapter will provide the methodological processes used to answer this question, first by detailing the theoretical framework that guided this investigation. The focus then shifts to the research methods and design for data collection, with participant observations and in-depth semi-structured interviews serving as the main source of data. The setting for the study will be described, along with participant sampling methods, and data-analysis tools and techniques. This chapter also addresses the role of the research, the topic of reciprocity, and ethical considerations.

Symbolic Interactionism as a Principal Methodological Framework

Blumer (1969) summarized the framework of symbolic interactionism in the following way:

> [It is a] down-to-earth approach to the scientific study of human group life and human conduct. Its empirical world is the natural world of such group life and conduct. It lodges its problems in this natural world, conducts its studies in it, and derives its interpretations from such naturalistic studies.
>
> (p. 47)

Blumer (1969) went on to say that symbolic interactionism is a distinctive way of categorizing and approaching the study of human group life and human behavior based on three premises:

> That human beings act toward things on the basis of the meanings that the things have for them ... such as individual independence or honesty, activities of others ... and such situations as an individual encounters in his daily life ... [The second premise is that] the meaning of such things

is derived from, or arises out of, the social interaction that one has with one's fellows, [and with other human beings. The third premise] is that these meanings are handled in, and modified through, an interpretive process used by the person in dealing with the things he encounters.

(p. 2)

A psychological analysis of human behavior, as perceived through the lens of symbolic interactionism, allows one to evaluate factors such as "stimuli, attitudes, conscious or unconscious motives, various psychological inputs, perception and cognition, and various features of personal organization to account for given forms or instances of human conduct" (Blumer, 1969, p. 3). Blumer asserted that human behavioral analysis relies on "such factors as social position, status demands, social roles, cultural prescriptions, norms and values, social pressures, and group affiliation" (p. 3).

Thus, interpreting human behavior is not only based on psychological processes, but also on the meanings derived in and through how people interact as social beings. In other words, social interactions become a medium through which the psychological and the sociological determinants of behavior intermingle to produce a particular form of human behavior.

According to Blumer (1969), three interrelated factors should be taken into account when working within a symbolic interactionism framework—all of which are germane to the formation of stigma and how that impacts beliefs and behaviors. First, people are inclined to act toward things (both external stimuli and other people) according to the meanings that they attach to themselves (their self), to events, and to other people. Second, meanings are developed via the ways that humans interact with each other in social situations. The third guiding principle is that these meanings are managed and can be altered as a result of the ways that humans interact with the objects and people with which/whom they come into contact.

Accordingly, this theoretical framework provides a logical foundation for the present study in that it allows for a deep understanding of the experiences of the self (i.e., of the PMI), the actions of the PO, the dynamic interactions between the PO and the PMI, and the role that stigma plays in each of these. Thus, symbolic interactionism was utilized herein to evaluate the meanings that PMIs make of their individual lived probation experiences. Additionally, sensitizing concepts were taken into consideration as to how an issue should be studied.

Sensitizing Concepts

Rather than pointing to specific attributes or benchmarks, sensitizing concepts provide the researcher with a general sense of reference and structure in how empirical issues should be studied. They suggest a direction along which to look and serve as interpretive tools in qualitative studies. One essential benefit of using sensitizing concepts in qualitative research is that they help to draw attention to essential features of social interaction in a particular social milieu. Another important benefit is that sensitizing concepts provide the means of seeing, sorting out, and understanding experience that helps with the emerging analysis of a study (Bowen, 2006).

Stigma and the possibility that PMIs perceive their interactions with POs as stigma-laden represents a sensitizing concept that (a) helped guide the data-collection processes, and (b) informed the evaluation of findings and subsequent analysis. This particular sensitizing concept also helped frame the research question, as well as the design of the interview protocols for both the PMIs and for POs.

Overall Strategy and Rationale

Qualitative "inquiry typically focuses in depth on relatively small samples, selected purposefully" (Coyne, 1997, p. 627). Since this approach is overwhelmingly used to think about and study social reality and experienced-based phenomena (McLeod, 2011), it has the potential to significantly contribute to the knowledge base of counseling, counselor education, psychological and behavioral sciences, and the criminal justice fields. Individual in-depth interviews and ethnographic observations are particularly efficacious ways of collecting qualitative data since they focus on capturing the individual lived experiences of people that can then be supplemented with other data (i.e., journaling, observations, and field notes) (Marshall & Rossman, 2011). For this study, qualitative approaches were used to elucidate the probation experiences of a select group of participants using *in vivo* references and direct accounts from POs and PMIs. The methodology employed herein facilitated a more nuanced understanding of the PMIs' experience with POs, with the ultimate goal of advancing social justice for this population through the authenticity of the findings reported herein (McLeod, 2011).

Participants' Recruitment and Study Setting

The 12 participants in this investigation were probationers and probation officers from the "North County Probation System" (NCPS) in "Newtown," located in a northeastern U.S. county of approximately 750,000 residents. (Both are pseudonyms for an actual county facility and town, which also happened to be the county seat.) The data-collection and research activities took place at this site. The sample of POs was drawn from a force of male and female probation officers. Male probationers in the North County Probation system were interviewed and included individuals of African, Latino, and

Caucasian descent, between ages 20 and 30 years. A total of 12 subjects, consisting of six probationers and six probation officers were interviewed.

In qualitative research, "sample selection has a profound effect on the ultimate quality of the research" (Coyne, 1997, p. 623). Sample selection is complex because of the many variations of sampling procedures and the overlapping nature of these sampling techniques. In fact, one criticism of a qualitative approach is that subjects are selected according to the "aims of the research [with] categories such as age, gender, status, role or function in [an] organization, stated philosophy or ideology serving as [the] starting points" (Coyne, 1997, p. 624). It is for this reason that a recurrent limitation of many qualitative studies is their applicability to larger populations.

Inclusion Criteria and Sampling

Due to the sizable population of all probation officers and probationers at the NCPS site, I utilized purposive sampling to help identify a manageable, yet representative, sample of subjects. The criteria used in identifying, recruiting, and selecting PMIs included the following: age (20–30 years of age); gender (male); having an existing mental health issue that required intensive mental health and/or substance abuse counseling; ability to attend two individual interviews and be available for a dyad observation; and ethnicity that reflected the breakdown of male offenders in this region (i.e., African American, Latino, or Caucasian). The criteria used in recruiting and selecting POs included the following: positioned as a specialty probation officer; availability for two in-depth interviews, and availability and willingness to be shadowed in an ethnographic observation.

The logic of purposive sampling lies in selecting information-rich cases for in-depth study. Information-rich cases are those from which one can learn a great deal about issues of central importance to goals of the research (Coyne, 1997; Patton, 1990). I also employed maximum variation, a type of purposive sampling where the researcher wants maximum variation in a sample and must decide what kinds of variations to maximize—and when. Typical variations include race, class, gender, or other person-related characteristics (Coyne, 1997). I also recruited with the intention of having maximum variation in the types of mental health diagnoses present in the cohort.

The gender of the subjects and selection of all male probationers for this study reflected the state gender breakdown of inmates, parolees, and probationers (males comprise 95.8% of committed male inmates and probationers in this northeastern U.S. state). There was no exclusion criterion from this study related to race/ethnicity. The race/ethnicity of the subjects reflected the breakdown of the probationer/PMI population in the NCPS, which is representative of this northeastern state's official demographics of inmates and probationers: 49.5% African Americans, 24% Hispanic, and 23.8% Caucasian. Another selection restriction was that all participants had to be able to understand the informed consent in English since (a) I read the consent forms out loud to each of the 12 participants, and (b) they had to read and understand the form in English before they could sign. Using only English-speaking subjects increased the efficiency of the interview protocols (interview and observations) and also facilitated the transcription and analysis of the data. It should also be noted that the selection process of the PMIs involved identification and recommendations from POs in order to capture as thoroughly as possible the intersubjective nature of the PO–PMI relationship. In other words, a dyadic recruitment process guided the recruitment and identification of eligible PMIs, which is detailed in a subsequent paragraph.

Recruitment Strategies

Recruitment commenced after gaining Institutional Review Board (IRB) approval and access to the site in April, 2015. The recruitment process began by first meeting with one of the administrators and with specialty POs who provide case management and rehabilitation services to PMIs. I met with the administrator, four probation officers, and two supervising probation officers. The POs who attended were identified as having an interest or availability to participate in the study. The supervising probation officers who attended the meeting shared that they were interested in gathering information about the study to share with their supervisees who were not in attendance. Supervising POs did not take part in the study. During the meeting I presented the focus and nature of the research, including the data-gathering components, along with a proposed timeline for the data-gathering phase of the endeavor. I introduced myself, described my role as the researcher, and shared my rationale for why I was interested in pursuing this investigation. I reviewed all of the components of the informational letter with the probation officers present, who were representative of different specialty divisions within the larger adult criminal services county probation department.

Each of the POs introduced themselves and their specialty affiliations within the department and we also talked about important themes related to expectations, commitments, and timing of the data-collection phase. We also discussed logistics and I was impressed with the ease and significance of the conversation; in fact, the POs demonstrated interest and attentiveness and asked some good questions (i.e., rationale and design of the study) that later impacted the next phases of subject selection. After fielding all of the questions and talking about scheduling and other logistical issues, I distributed the informed consent form and talked through the components of the form with the POs. Again, I read the form to ensure that everyone understood every phase of the process. Consents were presented and confirmed again during the initial interview sessions.

POs who agreed to take part were instrumental in identifying PMIs who met criteria for this study. Once PMIs were identified, I arranged an initial individual meeting with each of the identified individuals at a mutually agreeable time in the probation setting to explain the study and discuss the informed consent process. (Note that seven were initially recruited, but one was unable to take part due to eligibility criteria). This latter approach was efficacious in helping to identify potential probationers who met the inclusion criteria (i.e., male, 20–30 years of age, with a pre-existing mental health diagnosis). During the informed consent process with the PMIs, I explained the study and informed them that they could withdraw at any time and for any reason during the data-collection process (without being penalized for non-participation by their POs and from the probation system) with complete impunity—in other words, coercion played no role in participant selection or continued participation. I encouraged them to contact me if they had any questions about the study and made clear that they are not mandated to participate in this study. As a token of appreciation, at the end of the study each PMI participant who completed every phase of the study received a one-time $20 dollar gift card to Wal-Mart. The POs were not eligible for any payment due to established administrative policies and restrictions of accepting gifts as county government employees.

To reiterate, the POs were instrumental in identifying PMIs who met the criteria for the study. This process of selecting PMI-subjects was helpful in streamlining the identification of PMIs who were compliant in terms of attending appointments with their POs. Ultimately, PMIs who met the study criteria and successfully completed the initial screening process seemed more motivated (perhaps due to the fact that they were in compliance with other aspects of their treatment and rehabilitation protocols) and were generally able to complete the two-phase interview process (with one exception, as indicated earlier). This targeted selection process also enhanced subsequent data-collection processes. However, this selection process also potentially suggests that POs identified individuals who were intrinsically more compliant, which could indicate more supportive and positive probation/rehabilitation experiences. This linkage could also have impacted the types of narratives that PMIs shared about their relationships with their POs. This particular subject selection process is a limitation in the study and will be discussed in more detail in a later chapter.

Vulnerability of the Research Participants: PMIs

This study involved vulnerable subjects as defined by the Research Subjects Review Board (RSRB) guidelines for investigators. First, the probationer-subjects who were interviewed and observed were all facing legal sanctions and/or community sentences (i.e., these were offenders not sentenced to time in jail or prison, or they had had their sentences commuted) for crimes and violations of legal statutes. Second, at the time this study was conducted PMIs all had a DSM-IV-TR/DSM-5 diagnosable mental health condition for which they were receiving mental health and/or substance abuse treatment. I anticipated a potential vulnerability regarding the probation officers that could have resulted in employee sanctions if data was revealed with any identifiers. The way that they conduct their jobs is highly subjective and I was concerned that they would be reluctant to disclose any information inconsistent with policies (i.e., how they do their work as POs). To prevent potential sanctions and further vulnerability, I informed the POs that the data collected would be confidential and that names and other identifiers would be coded with pseudonyms.

Data Collection

In-depth Interviews as Design Strategy

The principal data-collection strategy was the use of one-on-one interviews with probationers and probation officers, which provided highly personal insights into the perspectives of both cohorts as they conceptualized their experiences with rehabilitation and treatment. Marshall and Rossman (2011) discussed the main benefits of using in-depth interviewing—it produces large amounts of data quickly and also serves as a co-constructed context of knowledge creation. The in-depth information that was gleaned from the individual interviews included access to information on "selected topics, personal histories, cultural knowledge and beliefs, [and] description of practices" (LeCompte & Schensul, 1999a, p. 128). This process enabled me to capture the subjects' own words through the use of open-ended questions that were flexible, which in some cases provided unexpected dimensions to the topic (Bogdan & Biklen, 2007).

Two rounds of interviews were conducted with all participants. Data from the first interviews, which were all audio-taped, were transcribed and coded prior to conducting the second interviews. To expedite data analysis, I utilized a professional transcription service for the audiotaped interviews that adhered to confidentiality standards related to the research. Each transcript was broken down into codes, after which the codes were grouped based on the similarities of themes. The second-round questions were more targeted and allowed the principal researcher to follow up on themes that emerged from the initial interviews.

Building rapport with participants, which was initiated during the screening process and continued through the interviews, augmented the comfort level and enhanced data collection. Additionally, I was always cognizant of the need to extend respect to every individual involved in this investigation, which is another strategy for building rapport (Blumer, 1969; Charmaz, 2006). Rapport was also established by my genuine interest in understanding the perspectives and actions of the subjects from a nonjudgmental standpoint (Charmaz, 2006).

Shadowing of POs and PMIs

The second strategy for obtaining data was through the use of selective shadowing and participant observations of the interactions between POs and PMIs. Observations allow one to capture situations as they occur, as well as help to generate more nuanced interpretations of the meanings of events and activities (LeCompte & Schensul, 1999b). Importantly, direct observations enable the researcher to gather triangulating data in relation to the other data-collection processes. Scollon and Scollon (2004) asserted that it is not enough to know what people *say* they do. The researcher must also determine the extent to which participant generalizations support the "reality" of what is being observed, since people often act very differently from what they say and how they act. Thus, first-hand observations of the interactions of selected participants provided a lens into the intricacies of PO–PMI interactions.

With little first-hand experience as to the particularities of supervision, I came to these shadowing opportunities with no other expectations except as an opportunity for me to learn and reflect on the probation experience. I selected dyads for observations that would provide rich data on probation and treatment experiences. Subjects were observed at the NCPS main office in Newtown. These information-rich cases were selected after the initial round of semi-structured interviews was completed and the resulting data was coded. I selected two dyads of PMI–PO from the larger pool of PMIs and selected two PMIs who shared that they were either in sustained recovery and remission of mental health issues/actively engaged in counseling and treatments, or indicated through their narratives that they were diligently working their recovery programs with some challenges (i.e., I also had to be mindful of the potential of PMIs' minimizing the problems they were experiencing in this interview context). These immersion/observations then provided an opportunity to discern the ways that PMIs' interactions and behaviors in their dyads reflect the styles/skills, attitudes, and disposition of both the PO and the PMI. There was no preset agenda for the observations; they were simply designed as an opportunity to immerse myself further in the context and begin to see the varied and diverse dynamics of supervision and the probation experience for PMIs with their POs. As a "participant-observer" in this process, my goal was to be able to "hear, see, and begin to experience reality as the participants do" (Marshall & Rossman, 2011, p. 140). The "how" and "what" of the observation meant that I had to prepare for the activities of probation supervision by mindfully being present to be engaged as an observer. In addition, in an attempt to capture and record the essence of these interactions, I used note-taking and recorded journal observations immediately after the activity finished. I organized the findings after the observation by noting the subjective and objective components of the experience and also indicated the plan and assessment of needs that occurred in the dyad supervision session. Notes and reflections were organized into a coherent picture of the activity immediately after the observation. Well-organized and reflective field notes represent important methods of data collection in this type of inquiry as they provide an immediate way of capturing participant observations, noting activities and interactions, and transforming them into functional sources of data (Marshall & Rossman, 2011).

The shadowing and observations took place at the same county probation office but on the third floor of the building, where cubicles and meeting spaces are available, with computers and a waiting area for the probationers. After reviewing the data from the initial interviews and cross-checking about the dyad assignments, I informed the probationers and POs in the two dyads I wanted to observe and shared my intent to shadow their supervision meeting. Consents were renegotiated and I again had to inform both entities about my role as a researcher and talked about other considerations (i.e., notetaking and my relatively non-participatory presence in the interview room). The observations of these supervision sessions lasted for a brief amount of time (about ten minutes) for the initial session and 20–25 minutes for the second interview. This time frame included the amount of time it took to wait for the start of the meeting in a general area to the culmination of the session.

Data Management

The data collected from interviews with six POs and six PMIs (during April/ May, 2015)—coupled with two participant observations—resulted in audio recordings, transcribed interviews, field notes, and journal notations (Scollon & Scollon, 2004). All data was maintained on an encrypted electronic storage device and accessed on a password-protected personal computer.

Triangulation of Data

The generation of multiple sources of data enables a researcher to triangulate those results, which represents an important strategy for confirming and corroborating the validity, credibility, and reliability of qualitative research (LeCompte & Schensul, 1999a). Indeed, studies that use only one means of data collection can be subject to criticism for lack of scientific rigor. Also, triangulation ensures that "information elicited from each key informant is corroborated by information from others—preferably people who have different perspectives on the subject or who occupy different positions in the project from initial informants" (p. 131). Triangulated data-collection processes also infer that "if one data set or source proves to be unreliable or incomplete, others will suffice to provide the information needed to answer each research question posed" (p. 131). Triangulation allows the researcher to elaborate on, check, or adjust the interpretations of the cultural scene in a continuing, recursive manner (LeCompte & Schensul, 1999a).

One important method in the triangulation of data is member checking, a strategy I utilized throughout the data-collection process. In this approach, I, as the researcher, actively sought opportunities to ask participants whether the documentation and interpretation of participant responses accurately reflected their intended meaning. During the second interviews with the PMIs and the POs, I provided summaries of notes/memos and tentative findings and asked for reactions, corrections, and further insights from participants, which then painted a fuller picture of their probation experiences.

Researcher Role

Bogdan and Biklen (2007) wrote of the need for the investigator to consider his/her identity and position in relation to study subjects, since this has implications for the ways the researcher structures the investigation, negotiates fieldwork, and interprets findings. Issues like class, race/ethnicity, status, and educational attainment can have a powerful influence on subjects and for the data-collection processes. In my position of "power" as the investigator, I was ever cognizant that the probationers might be dissuaded from full disclosure based on a perceived power differential between them and myself—coupled with the possible concern that their confidential information could get back to their PO. Thus, it was important to use the informed consent process as a way to mediate the power differentials, reinforce the promise of confidentiality, and to be open and honest about the study and the potential implications of the findings for participants and more broadly for the field. Additionally, by encouraging participants to ask questions about the study and its processes it demystified the research and provided participants with a voice even before the first interview. Finally, the researcher as participant-observer, collecting ethnographic data and using constant comparative analysis, creates an inevitable risk for bias in the interpretation of the data. This challenge for bias to overshadow the experience of a participant-observer is a general issue that is cross-contextual in qualitative research. It is a consideration that required constant awareness on my part in this data-collection setting and subsequently during the conceptualizing of the findings.

Trustworthiness Criteria for Qualitative Research

There are proven ways to ensure the credibility, transferability, dependability, and confirmability of findings in qualitative research—in other words, that the data and resultant findings are relevant and accurate (Marshall & Rossman, 2011). Multiple strategies are employed to strengthen the trustworthiness of qualitative data: (a) by minimizing any discrepancies between participant understanding and researcher interpretations; (b) to ensure that the research is sufficiently thick and rich to be applied to other contexts, settings, and situations; (c) to ensure the consistency of findings; and (d) to mediate any researcher bias (Marshall & Rossman, 2011). Such safeguards include considering the length of qualitative data collection (i.e., making sure the data-collection timeline will allow for data saturation, and being persistent in the types of observations needed for thick/rich evidence. In studies for which the time frame for collecting data may be short (perhaps due to financial constraints), the researcher must ensure that this potential limitation does not challenge the trustworthiness of the data (further described in the limitations section). Other proven methods for enhancing reliability include triangulating data collection and analysis (e.g., via reflective journaling and field notes), peer debriefing, and member checking. For this investigation, peer debriefing was utilized to ascertain the relative accuracy of coding schemes and the tentative theoretical interpretations that were formulated prior to the final analyses and write-up. Finally, I as the Principal Investigator explored my own biases in order to interpret and report results as dispassionately as possible. Reflective journaling, used throughout the data-collection phases of the research, helped in building my awareness and facilitated insights about my role, influence, and helped to identify and work through some of the blind spots that could have impacted my navigations at the site as a researcher.

Ethical Considerations

Several ethical issues related to methods of data collection were addressed in this study. With regard to participant observations, there is the issue of respect. The POs and PMIs who took part in this study (both in interviews and during observations) were made fully aware of the intent and methodology of this investigation; this was detailed orally and through the informed consent forms. The POs and PMIs were considered full partners in this research process and I actively sought opportunities to acknowledge their contributions and participation (Marshall & Rossman, 2011). It should also be noted that the informed consent forms were re-presented during the shadowing and participant observation phase of data collection, which ensured that the participants understood my role as an observer in that particular context.

There were also potential ethical issues related to the individual interviews that emerged, such as the relationship dynamics between the researcher and the interviewee, reciprocity, and the potential for emotional challenges related to types of personal information they shared. To manage these concerns, it was important to (a) stress both orally and in writing that all data would be kept strictly confidential to protect the interviewee's identity throughout the data-collection and data-reporting processes, and (b) to make sure that the relationship would be non-manipulative and reciprocal to the greatest extent possible (Marshall & Rossman, 2011). Finally, I ensured that PMIs had access to their treatment providers and POs as a precaution against potential psychological strain that could have resulted from the questions and discussions in the individual interviews.

Analytical Framework

Grounded Theory

Grounded theory was used as the principal data-collection and analytical tool; this approach facilitates the use of "flexible guidelines for collecting and analyzing [rich] qualitative data to [help] construct theories 'grounded' in the data themselves" (Charmaz, 2006, p. 2). Through the use of qualitative coding, I separated, sorted, and synthesized data into logical categories that allowed me to compare and contrast the relationships between the data. The process of checking and refining the data produced emerging categories that culminated in a grounded theory, or an "abstract theoretical understanding of the studied experience" (Charmaz, 2006, pp. 3–4). This analytical process allowed for the development of strong grounded theories generated from the rich data obtained from in-depth interviews, observations, and field notes.

There is an acknowledgement in qualitative research about the influence of the reflective lens of the researcher. Charmaz (2006) asserted that the researcher is not a passive receptacle "into which data [is] poured ... Researchers and research participants make assumptions about what is real, possess stocks of knowledge, occupy social statuses, and pursue purposes that influence their respective views and actions in the presence of each other" (p. 15). The researcher also spoke to the "social actions that researchers construct in concert with others in particular places and times ... We interact with data and create theories about it ... We do not exist in a vacuum" (Charmaz, 2006, p. 129).

With this understanding in mind, constructivist grounded theory was useful for the process of data collection and analysis, principally because it looks at how individuals view their situation and acknowledges that meaning is ascribed subjectively. It examines the how, when, and to "what extent the studied experience is embedded in larger and often, hidden positions, networks, situations, and relationships" (Charmaz, 2006, p. 130). Charmaz also reiterated that constructivist grounded theory analysis is

> contextually situated in time, place, culture, and situation. Because constructivists see facts and values as linked, they acknowledge that what they see—and don't see—rests on values. Thus, constructivists attempt to become aware of their presuppositions and to grapple with how they affect the research. They realize that grounded theorists can ironically import preconceived ideas into their work when they remain unaware of their starting assumptions. Thus, constructivism fosters researchers' reflectivity about their own interpretations as well as those of their research participants.
>
> (2006, p. 131)

In short, the constructivist researcher holds that "knowledge is constructed rather than discovered [and that] the world we know is a particularly human construction" (Stake, 1995, pp. 99–100). With this role, the constructivist researcher's "view encourages providing readers with good raw material for their own generalizing" (Stake, 1995, p. 102) and seeks to construct knowledge by interpreting experiential data. With this perspective, I formulated findings that I hope explicate the experiences of PMIs relative to POs within this probation context.

Data Analytical Tools

Charmaz (2006) defined coding as a means of "naming segments of data with a label that simultaneously categorizes, summarizes and accounts for each piece of data. Coding is the first step in moving beyond concrete statements in the data to making analytic interpretations" (p. 43) about the data. Assigning qualitative codes leads to the selection, separation, and sorting of data, all of which are essential for the development of theoretical categories. For this investigation I used grounded theory coding schemes as mechanisms for developing an integrated process of data analysis. Specifically, this process enabled me to identify emerging themes from the data; coding also allowed me to compare and contrast the findings with the theoretical framework used to conceptualize this investigation.

The initial phase of grounded theory–based coding involves categorizing "words, lines, or segments of data followed by a focused, selective phase that uses the most significant or frequent initial codes to sort, synthesize, integrate, and organize large amounts of data" (Charmaz, 2006, p. 46). During this first coding phase, I looked for "action words/segments" that reflected actual probation actions. This deliberate coding scheme reduced the tendency toward making unsubstantiated conceptual leaps ahead of the analytical process through the development of provisional and comparative discoveries that were clearly grounded in the data. In addition, the use of action words and quotes to describe the data emphasized the "words and actions of respondents, preserve[d] the fluidity of their experience and [provided] new ways of looking at [the data]" (Charmaz, 2006, p. 49). This strategy provided a means of reflecting the participants' experiences as opposed to using an outsider's perspective to describe the phenomenon. There were potentialities in using these proven techniques as a way to facilitate this initial coding process, including

> breaking the data up into their component parts or properties, defining the actions on which they rest, looking for tacit assumptions, explicating implicit actions and meanings, crystallizing the significance of the points, comparing data with data, and identifying gaps in the data.
>
> (Charmaz, 2006, p. 50)

One proven method of coding is line-by-line coding, which enables the researcher to draw comparisons between data in the field notes and the potential utility of analytical categories and critical processes. Additionally, *in vivo* coding was used, which involves highlighting or excerpting the actual words/phrases of participants when they reflect or capture a key theme or element (Charmaz, 2006; Marshall & Rossman, 2011).

The types of data that I collected included factual incidents gained from comparing incidents with incidents, which allowed for the identification of emerging concepts. The repetitive process also allowed for constant comparison of data between and among participant observations and interviews to find similarities and differences. In addition, it facilitated a co-constructed reality in that the findings reflected my perspective of what occurred and the understandings and logic of the participants (Charmaz, 2006).

The second analytical process used in the coding scheme was focused coding, which is "more directed, selective, and conceptual than word-by-word, line-by-line, and incident-by-incident coding" (Charmaz, 2006, p. 57). Focused coding facilitates the synthesis and extrapolation of larger segments of data by which "new threads for analysis become apparent ... Events, interviews, and perspectives come into analytic purview that [were] not thought of before. [Consequently,] focused coding check[s] preconceptions about the topic" (Charmaz, 2006, p. 59).

There were also instances in the data analysis when categories needed to be compared and related to other categories or subcategories. Axial coding served as an important research tool in clarifying relationships around the axis of a category. This approach allowed me as the researcher to sort, synthesize, and organize large amounts of data and reassemble them in new ways after open coding (Charmaz, 2006).

The final coding scheme that was implemented is theoretical coding. According to Charmaz (2006), theoretical coding is a sophisticated level of coding that conceptualizes and specifies possible relationships between categories developed during the focused coding phase. Theoretical coding is integrative and "may help lead from the focused codes ... But also moves [the] analytic story in a theoretical direction" (Charmaz, 2006, p. 63). When applied appropriately, theoretical coding adds clarity and provides substantive, coherent, and comprehensive analytical processes to describe the phenomenon of interest.

It must be noted that a potential problematic issue in coding qualitative data is the possibility of forcing preconceived themes onto the data through researcher bias (Charmaz, 2006). In other words, as a person with knowledge of the population and the phenomena under scrutiny, my assumptions and preconceptions could influence data analysis. However, the tools described above (e.g., self-reflective journaling, peer debriefing, and data triangulation) helped to circumvent this possibility.

Data Analysis Procedures

As recommended by Marshall and Rossman (2011), data analysis is sufficient "when critical categories are defined, relationships between them are established, and they are integrated into an elegant, credible interpretation" (p. 209). For this investigation, data analysis consisted of organizing the data, immersing myself in the data, working on generating categories and themes, coding the data, offering interpretations through analytic memos, searching for alternative understandings, and writing up preliminary results (Marshall & Rossman, 2011). Once the data collection yielded redundant patterns and little could be gained from collecting additional data (i.e., I reached saturation), I worked on evaluating and searching the "themes, typologies, and patterns in [the] data for negative instances of the patterns, [which were then incorporated into developed constructs]" (Marshall & Rossman, 2011, p. 220).

Marshall and Rossman (2011) also asserted that when beginning an analysis it is imperative that the researcher spends time organizing the findings (i.e., using note cards as an organizational tool; performing minor editing; and generally cleaning what seems overwhelming and unmanageable). Specifically, they recommended that the researcher log the types of data according to the dates and times when, the places where, and the persons from whom they were gathered. Writing about qualitative data cannot be separated from the analytic process. In choosing words to summarize and reflect the complexity of the data, the researcher is engaging in interpretive acts and shaping the volumes of raw data. Marshall and Rossman also noted the following:

> Into the various phases of data analysis and report writing are woven considerations of the soundness, usefulness, and ethical conduct of the qualitative research study. Some consideration should be given to the value, truthfulness, and soundness of the study throughout the design of the proposal (p. 222). [In addition] considerations of role, for example, should address the personal biography of the researcher and how that might shape events and meanings.
>
> (p. 210)

The varied data obtained from interviews with POs and PMIs, observations, and field notes were continuously analyzed and examined between and among groups. Evidence that supported a consensus of findings were grouped and analyzed together and outlying data were cross-examined and labeled as potential negative case examples.

Units of Analyses and Use of Qualitative Software

For the purposes of this study, the PMIs and POs served as the units of analyses. The data gleaned from observing and interviewing the PMIs and the POs served as dyadic data, which was helpful in understanding the experiences of the PMIs relative to their experiences with their POs. Moreover, their social interactions as obtained via direct observations of two dyads served as a complementary unit of analysis to the analysis of self and the actions of the individual participants.

I used the NVivo 10 Qualitative software to store, manage, analyze, and code the data obtained from all sources. This software was also used to write detailed analytical memos. Once the initial drafts of the analytical memos were completed, I transferred them to a word-processing document for further cleaning. All of the preliminary and written data and analysis were initially saved on an encrypted flash drive and then imported, transferred, and uploaded into the NVivo software database for analyses.

Findings are presented in Chapter 4.

Chapter Summary

This chapter provided a detailed description of the qualitative research framework and specific methods used in this investigation. To reiterate, a symbolic interactionist paradigm served as a guiding framework, while grounded theory provided a foundation for interpreting the data. This chapter also included a discussion of sampling strategies, methods of data collection and analyses, the role of the researcher, and ethical considerations. Chapter 4 provides the results of this investigation, which in many cases are supported by quotes from participants.

References

Blumer, H. (1969). *Symbolic interactionism: Perspective and method*. Englewood Cliffs, NJ: Prentice Hall.

Bogdan, R. C., & Biklen, S. K. (2007). *Qualitative research for education: An introduction to theories and methods*. Boston, MA: Pearson Education, Inc.

Bowen, G. A. (2006). Grounded theory and sensitizing concepts. *International Journal of Qualitative Methods*, 5(3), 1–9.

Charmaz, K. (2006). *Constructing grounded theory: A practical guide through qualitative analysis*. Sage: Thousand Oaks, CA.

Coyne, I. T. (1997). Sampling in qualitative research: Purposeful and theoretical sampling; merging or clear boundaries. *Journal of Advanced Nursing*, 26, 623–630.

LeCompte, M. D., & Schensul, J. J. (1999a). Collecting ethnographic data. In M. D. LeCompte and J. J. Schensul (Eds.), *Designing and conducting ethnographic research*, (pp. 127–146). Lanham, MD: Altamira Press.

LeCompte, M. D., & Schensul, J. J. (1999b). Data analysis: How ethnographers make sense of their data. In M. D. LeCompte and J. J Schensul (Eds.), *Designing and conducting ethnographic research* (pp. 147–159). Lanham, MD: Altamira Press.

Marshall, C., & Rossman, G. (2011). *Designing qualitative research*, fifth edition. London: Sage.

McLeod, J. (2011). *Qualitative research in counseling and psychotherapy*, second edition. Thousand Oaks, CA: Sage.

Patton M. Q. (1990). *Qualitative evaluation and research methods*, second edition. Newbury Park, CA: Sage.

Scollon, R., & Scollon, S. (2004). *Nexus analysis: Discourse and the emerging internet*. London: Routledge.

Stake, R. (1995). *The art of case study research*. London: Sage.

3 Results

Description of the Setting

The setting for the data collection must be described, since (a) it may have played a role in how PMIs experienced probation with their POs, and (b) it offered additional opportunities for observing probation staff as they went about their duties. The interview room/space that I was assigned for all data-collection sessions at the North County Probation System in Newtown was a private space with a door, which ensured that all conversations would remain confidential. A security guard was always within view. It should also be noted that this private office featured an audio intercom, which was used to page probation officers when needed; this system was utilized rather consistently, thus adding to the noise and chatter from the adjacent waiting room, as well as sometimes interrupting the flow of conversation. Additionally, on several occasions I, as an unnoticed bystander, had opportunities to observe activities that were occurring at the site. Throughout both serendipitous opportunities and scheduled interviews/observations with PMIs and PO, I detailed my observations and recollections in a series of field notes—either as the activity was occurring or later that same day.

PMIs' Demographics and Nature of Needs

The PMIs interviewed for this study featured a range of psychiatric and psychosocial issues that specifically contributed to their criminal activity, probation sentences, and mandate to engage in specialized mental health and substance abuse treatments. Demographic data was obtained in individual interviews with each of the PMIs and also noted via observations of the PO–PMI dyads. Among the PMIs who participated in this study, three were Caucasian, one was African-American, one was Hispanic, and one identified as Puerto Rican and Black. The self-reported mental health challenges among this group of PMIs included mood and bipolar disorders, anxiety disorders, substance use disorders, and other co-occurring medical health conditions. The counseling interventions reported within this group of PMIs included participation in weekly individual and group counseling, taking regimens of psychotropic medications, and active participation in Narcotics Anonymous and other self-help meetings in the local community. The PMIs who took part in this study were generally in compliance and seemed largely agreeable about the need to engage in drug and alcohol and mental health counseling, and to continue to engage in other forms of supportive recovery oriented and self-help meetings (i.e., Narcotics and Alcoholics Anonymous). Indeed, these six men conceptualized their treatment experiences (although mandated) as a critical part of their lives.

Results from Interviews with Probationers with Mental Illness

The results of this study are based on data from (a) the initial and second-round semi-structured interviews that were completed with both PMIs and POs, and (b) the two live observations between selected PMIs and POs dyads. Where information revealed in an interview might allow respondents to be identified by other respondents within the system, a simple identification as either PMI or PO is used. When information is general enough not to reveal identity, PMIs and POs are identified based, in both cases, on a lettering system of a–f. Data garnered from interviews and observations facilitated data triangulation, and offered a varied perspective of the phenomena of probation as well.

Reflective journals and peer debriefing helped to facilitate the data and coding schemes used to analyze and make sense of all data. These processes (i.e., using a journal) included writing about my thoughts of how the data and data analyses were coming together, and also allowed for a deepened understanding of the patterns and themes that were found in the accumulated data. A number of significant theoretical and practical themes emerged from a careful synthesis of the interview transcripts and observations, which while not exhaustive, do stand out as the most significant results confirmed by these multiple data sources. The following initial analytic and thematic codes were gleaned from the interview transcripts prior to the development of the final themes. The narratives and transcript data from the PMIs includes the following initial codes and impressions grounded in and from the data:

1 PMIs' impressions of the benefits of probation.
2 PMIs' impressions of the probationer–PO relationship.
3 PMIs' impressions of POs and perceived benefits.
4 PMIs' impressions of treatment and rehabilitation.
5 PMIs' impressions of reporting expectation and impact.
6 PMIs' impressions of mental health issues and treatment.

Initial codes were generated after carefully reviewing the transcripts in the initial and second round of interviews and looking for thematic clues and instances where narratives showed a consistent and repetitive pattern across the different participants' reports. Again, these patterns were primarily a reflection of the protocols used in the data-collection phase of the research. After these thematic clues for both PMIs and POs (see subsequent paragraphs) were identified, I drafted and summarized the findings and themes through the use of analytic memos, which formed the basis for the sections of the findings detailed in this chapter. In addition, there were particular *in vivo* codes that were carefully selected, which arguably reflects the themes in individual categories of findings about the phenomenon of probation (i.e., from the perspective of the PMIs and the POs). Observational findings are used as a secondary frame of reference, particularly to help provide a different perspective of the phenomenon of probation provided in the interviewing component of the data-collection processes. The observational data were integrated into the final analyses by focusing on how the reports gained from talking about probation and its benefits and effects differed and are substantiated by what actually happened in a live interaction. Findings from the shadowing/observations were not coded line by line or through *in vivo* coding, but evaluated as themes that confirmed or disconfirmed the evidence collected in the interviews.

The initial reporting of findings is focused on the findings from PMIs and focused on the sets of themes gained from a careful synthesis of the categories of codes provided above. These themes in the final analyses and findings contain some disconfirming, negative case examples among the data generated from the PMI-respondents, indicating that some divergent views emerged from the PMI-respondents. Generally, however, a clear conceptualization emerged of PMIs' probationary experiences, which is depicted in Figure 3.1 and summarized according to three overarching areas and their ancillary themes:

1 PMIs' perception of probation as rehabilitation and renewal:

    a   PMIs' professed belief that probation and treatment mandates improve their mental health.

    b   PMIs' professed belief that probation facilitates sobriety and recovery.

    c   PMIs' professed belief that probation facilitates improved behaviors.

2 PMIs' relationship with and perception of POs:

    a   PO perceived as an ally.

    b   PO perceived as a mentor.

    c   PO perceived support based on contingencies.

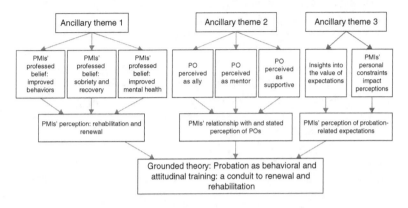

Figure 3.1 Thematic representation of PMI experiences.

3 PMIs' perception of probation-related expectations (i.e., reporting schedules):

    a   Insights into the value of expectations and conditioning.

    b   PMIs' personal constraints impact perceptions of value of probation conditioning.

Theme 1: PMIs' Perception of Probation as Rehabilitation and Renewal

The PMI-respondents agreed that probation encouraged rehabilitation and renewal via three important avenues: (a) it facilitated their engagement in treatment, (b) it encouraged them, through the structure offered, to adhere to services related to self-care and recovery, and (c) it promoted activities that prevented relapse to pathological behaviors. Principally, the PMIs lauded their engagement in counseling, which encouraged the development of self-preserving attitudes and behaviors (e.g., dealing with substance abuse issues), and addressed their specific mental health issues. The PMIs appeared to buy into the notion that treatment works and will continue to facilitate positive change. The following ancillary themes support their notion that probation serves as a source of rehabilitation and renewal.

Ancillary Theme 1a: PMIs' Professed Belief that Probation and Treatment Mandates Improved Their Mental Health

    "So I understand just how important treatment is and keeping up with it."
                                                (PMI-E, Interview 1)

There were various opportunities during the first and second round of interviews to talk with PMIs about the process of probation and its outcomes. One probationer described several positive impacts of probation—but especially receiving assistance with housing, which enhanced his sense of safety and normalcy. Combined with a steady medication regimen, the possibility of having a room of his own increased this man's sense of optimism. Another PMI discussed how a suicide attempt opened his PO's eyes after which time many services fell into place, thus pointing to the benefits of probation from a social services perspective. One PMI elaborated on some of the social service resources:

Q: What are some of the highs and the lows of being on probation? So, for example, what are some of the benefits you get out of being on probation? PMI-F: I got to see my case manager and go to DSS and grab a landlord statement, fill it out (Interview 1).

Responses of PMIs generally indicated that they were expected to engage in specialized counseling experiences as a condition of their probation sentences—and POs monitored PMIs' progress in treatment using a variety of methods, which will be detailed later in this chapter. One PMI described the nature and intensity of his mental health sessions, along with additional treatment dynamics.

Mental health counseling, I go once a week … Mostly, we talk about … how my week was. [Are] there any pressing issues that happened over the last week that you really need to talk to me about? How are your medicines working? You have any suicidal thoughts? Are you depressed, anxious? [It's the] same thing every week.

(PMI-A, Interview 1)

In addition to reporting expectations with POs, all of the PMIs interviewed in this study had a range of treatment and rehabilitation expectations that they were mandated to participate in weekly. PMI-A's statement that "it's the same thing every week" could be interpreted in two ways: (a) that the repetition and expected nature of treatment intervention is boring and monotonous, thus leading to disengagement, or (b) repetition was helping this particular individual to be constantly diligent about taking care of his mental health and addressing depressive, anxious, and potentially serious suicidal tendencies. PMI-A reported that he participated in substance abuse treatment, and detailed how his weekly chemical-dependency treatment sessions were structured:

For the drug and alcohol rehab, there's like eight or ten of us in a group. We have check-ins. The check-ins are your name, your clean date, how you're feeling and why, a positive trait about you, how much nicotine

you've had in the last week, and do you need any group time. Like if you
have any issues you want to talk to the group about.

(PMI A-Interview 1)

Thus, the evidence here seems to support the value of repetitive types of
experiences that this particular PMI (and potentially others) have to adhere
to on a regular basis.

Conversely, when perceived through a different lens, the monotony and
familiarity inherent in these types of experiences could lead to apathy, where
the individual is just going through the motions. Nonetheless, such monotony could be construed as a critical part of conditioning and training that
the evidence shows is happening. By following the rules and regulations of
probation and the mandates of treatment providers, the PMI is deferring his
authority to make independent decisions about what healthy behavior means.
He is then forced to adhere to the authority and power of the criminal justice
system, the mental health system, and the overall mandate of the judge. One
probationer reported how he meets his treatment mandate:

Q: How do you kind of meet the requirements of probation? What do
you have to do?

PMI: The only thing that [is] really mandated or expected of me is to continue with my mental health treatment.

This narrative snapshot captures the necessity to engage in services that PMI-E
and others are mandated to engage in as a condition of their probation sentences.

As summarized above, most of the PMIs had both substance use and mental health disorders and engaged in structured weekly treatments. A number of the men shared certain insights about their conditions and voiced the
importance of treatment. For example, one PMI shared that he had been
experiencing "all kinds of disorders since [he] was a child ... and [under-
stood] just how important treatment is and keeping up with it" (Interview 1).
The mandate to engage in counseling provided added motivations to follow
the requirements of probation—and when followed to the letter, reduced the
possibility of conflict between the PMIs and POs.

Probation requirements also typically included finding a job and in some
cases working toward obtaining their General Equivalency Degrees (GED).
However, one probationer shared that his PO supported him by minimizing the
pressure to juggle too much. This pressure could have set the PMI up for failure:

As of right now, it's just focus on these two things, [work and treatment]
and then go from there. They just don't want to put like a hundred things
on my plate and then get overwhelmed and then have something bad

happen. They just want, you know, it's [many years of probation], so we can take baby steps to get where we need to go.

(PMI, Interview 1)

This quote points to the importance of a PO's sensitivity in recognizing how much the PMI can handle. Thus, to some extent the two parties have to agree on the activities and events that must be completed/addressed during probation. In other words, PMIs have personal investments and goals that make these conditioning and training processes a lot more collaborative and fluid. Another PMI noted that he was working towards his GED and often spoke about how motivated, capable, and engaged he was in this pursuit as part of his treatment and rehabilitation plan. One PMI described his GED program in the following way:

It's a wonderful program. I recommend it to anybody who is serious about their future as far as working because they offer trades there. [They work with] anybody who [is] serious about getting their high school equivalency diploma.

(PMI, Interview 1)

This kind of narrative indicates that the probation experience for the PMI can be a complex, multi-faceted plan that entails more than medication checks. PMI-D provides evidence of the behavioral and attitudinal conditioning that probation sentences usually involve. There was a general agreement among all the PMIs that "fixing" a mental health and/or substance abuse issue involved other probation-mandated changes. PMI-D discussed the maturation processes that were expected of the probationer as a result of pro-social skills building and education:

[You] know. I was young, [and] a lot of things were distracting me. I was immature. I didn't have the information then that I have now, so I don't blame myself, you know. I just accepted who I was then versus who I am now.

(PMI-D, Interview 1)

He added,

I have [grown] and matured, you understand what I'm saying? When you're a kid, you think like that, you understand what I'm saying? But if you're an adult and you're still thinking like that, then you haven't matured much.

(PMI-D Interview 1)

Mental health counseling and substance abuse treatment encouraged the six probationers who took part in this study to think differently about the problems they had and were experiencing. These treatment protocols helped to reduce the cognitive and behavioral barriers that in the past had led to inappropriate behaviors through poor reasoning. And the conditioning and training offered by POs and counseling practitioners facilitated these processes (i.e., developing and strengthening the ego and helping to facilitate insights).

This section provides some perspectives into how these PMI-respondents thought about their mental health treatment and the ways that mandated treatment and rehabilitation services impacted them and their decision-making abilities. The statements supporting Ancillary Theme 1a indicate that probation-mandated treatment and related services (e.g., education and housing assistance) had positive outcomes on PMIs and facilitated maturation, growth, and optimism. Moreover, their comments suggest that PMIs have bought into and are cognizant of what must be done to prevent issues related to non-compliance, and they endeavored to avoid non-participation and non-engagement.

Ancillary Theme 1b: PMIs' Professed Belief that Probation Facilitates Sobriety and Recovery

"But if I do something with that thought and I change that thought and I change it into something positive I know I could—like if I run to a meeting and go talk about it, like about my addiction, I know I'm not going to use that day. That's what I [try] to do."

(PMI-C, Interview 1)

The PMIs described a number of challenges connected to their mental health treatment and chemical use management. Although a requirement of probation, most talked about the value of intensive treatment as a source of support and expectation. The components of treatment also served as a personal plan for improved health and wellbeing, which was expedited via their helping relationship with their POs. The six PMIs who took part in this study described similar strategies for addressing sobriety and recovery: attending meetings like Narcotics Anonymous (NA), being vigilant about the potential dangers of "people, places, and things" (a notion that all recovery addicts try to keep in mind in managing and maintaining their abstinence), and having a positive cognitive and behavioral repertoire on which to rely in times of distress. One PMI talked about the challenges of staying sober and his use of cognitive skills to counter self-destructive thoughts that would otherwise lead to relapse.

But if I had stopped doing the things I'm doing now to get [to] where I'm at, it could always come back up. Like if I'm thinking about it, if I'm thinking about using and I just keep thinking about it and don't do nothing about that thought, I'm going to end up going to use again because that's all I know. But if I do something with that thought and I change that thought and I change it into something positive, I know I could— like if I run to a meeting and go talk about it, like about my addiction, I know I'm not going to use that day.

(PMI-C, Interview 1)

For this probationer, remaining clean involved a conscious relapse prevention plan (attending meetings facilitated through probation) and a change of attitude.

One PMI spoke about the need to be vigilant and careful of distractions as a component of his rehabilitation, recovery, and mental health. He reported the value of knowing about the consequences of repeating mistakes—especially with respect to his relationship with his children and noted that not making mistakes was a source of ongoing motivation. PMI-D underscored the need to surround himself with people who will positively influence him.

I don't use drugs anymore, so knowing what I want in life, trying my hardest to stay away from those who don't want better for me from those whose life is rough, you know, because it's easy for them to like you, you know. [You all] are not going through the same things in life. Or [you all] haven't been through the same things in life. So, you know, they may want to be your friend and, you know, [want to] be around you all the time and stuff like that, you know. And they'll distract you from what you want to, you know, so over the years I've been trying my hardest to stay away from those kinds of people, who would distract me from, you know, obtaining what I would like to obtain.

(Interview 1)

Another PMI also talked about the value of vigilance and having outside supports (i.e., outside of treatment and rehabilitation) to help guide his recovery process. In fact, he reiterated the importance of his daily fight and focus on sobriety—even over his expectations and familial commitments.

Now on the weekends, I'm off trying to find something else to do, maybe hang out at my family's house for a little while. Like this Saturday, I think my [relative's] got a little meeting to see what we want to do for [the holiday]. But I know there's going to probably be drinking over there, but [like] the saying at AA is "If you don't belong, don't be long," so I'm not going to be that long if I know it's going to be stuff around that I don't want to be around, because I'm not going to let it hinder my sobriety because my sobriety has to come first.

The evidence from these quotes indicates the level of psychological and behavioral commitment the PMI must make toward his treatment and recovery. These narratives also paint a picture of the ways PMIs conceptualize their day-to-day goal of staying clean and sober from substance abuse, which probably contributed to their criminal justice involvement. Similarly, PMI-C confirmed that probation facilitated his ongoing sobriety. He talked about the value of meeting people who were also sober, learning that having fun can be achieved without substance abuse, and building up a supportive network of like-minded individuals.

> Today I try to live a full life and to the fullest, and I don't have to smoke weed or drink beer or drink bottles just to have fun. You could have fun sober, and some of the meetings show us that.
>
> (Interview 1)

Interestingly, this probationer later shared his experiences of a prior probation sentence when he was an adolescent in the system, and he compared and contrasted his current experience with the previous probation. He now appeared to be able to see the benefits of being on probation and focusing on his health and wellbeing. He described that when he was younger he had other intentions and did not care as much as he does now. The realization now is that he knows he has a problem and seemed able to want to work towards change. In reflecting on the two probationary experiences, PMI-C asserted that he had changed. He attributed his better outlook and improved insight to having a different mindset now and being more psychologically and behaviorally mature. As an older, more experienced probationer, he now appeared to inculcate what he learned in meetings about the value of staying clean.

Ancillary Theme 1c: PMIs' Professed Belief that Probation Facilitates Improved Behaviors

> "I'm doing good. I've got almost six months clean … I'm looking into volunteer work somewhere."
>
> (PMI Interview 1)

Many of the probationers described early mental health challenges, as well as how exposure to drugs and alcohol affected them. They also reported that early issues in adolescence resulted in crime and their involvement in the criminal justice system. In spite of those early challenges, many of the probationers spoke with optimism about how their current probation and improved decision-making via counseling and related interventions was helping to turn their lives around—for example, in the case of this PMI:

> Like being dependent on [drugs] and being addicted to it from ... [my early teens] to my late 20s, like I just didn't find a way out. But I had [a couple of] years sober ... and then I just became complacent, stopped going to meetings and stopped being around supportive people. And then I went back out for a little while, been coming in and out.
>
> (PMI, Interview 1)

One PMI recalled his early introduction to cannabis, alcohol, and tobacco early in high school; he made a connection between his drug use and ultimately dropping out of school. I asked this PMI about how chemical dependency issues he had in adolescence impacted his choices to engage in criminal behavior. At this point in his recovery, he described how he was able to reflect on his history and on the damage that drugs and alcohol had on his health, prior decision-making, and criminal behavior:

Question: Do you think that the marijuana thing is really the primary reason why you even got involved with the criminal justice system in the first place, or do you have other kind of behaviors that cause[d] you to get involved in the criminal justice system?

PMI: I think it plays a big part in it ... Yeah, because if I wasn't under the influence or if it wasn't around or if I didn't have it, I don't think I would be in the criminal justice system. Like, I caught my first charge [as a minor] ... It was something minor, but I still caught it. I was [a minor]. Then my second charge was ... when I got dropped in jail. ... I basically was just trying to find money to feed my habit. But I was young at the time. I was [a minor], and like, if I didn't see a pattern by that time, I didn't know I had an addiction then. But then it progressed over the years, but now I know I've got a problem.

Based on his interview session, this PMI attributed his enhanced psychological maturity and more positive attitude to the benefits of probationary training and conditioning.

Similarly, another PMI talked about the challenges of having mental health issues since he was a child. He reiterated the importance of his continued engagement in mental health treatment and maintaining his medication regimen.

I mean, I've been on medications, like strong medications … and stuff, since I was literally [a young child], so I've had … all kinds of disorders since I was a child. So I understand just how important treatment is and keeping up with it.

For these men, probation-mandated treatment options provided more structured ways to cope with mental illness and helped them abstain from substance misuse—both of which facilitated enhanced decision making.

PMI-D recalled growing up as a disenfranchised youth with minimal opportunities and a rough life. In fact, most of these probationers (if not all) had a difficult family life and experienced other psychosocial challenges that led them down a trajectory of deviance and crime, in addition to drug and/or alcohol abuse. Nonetheless, PMI-D claimed that he was capable of learning new behaviors.

I mean, my upbringing was rough. It was rough, you know what I mean? And you know, people get incarcerated based on really their upbringing being rough, you know what I mean? That's not helping them. Let's get some help for this young man or this young lady. Let's not lock them up, you know what I mean? They're just locking people up, you know what I mean. I'm never going to be too old to learn, you know what I mean?

PMI-D also spoke of the value of probation as an opportunity for changing behaviors through positive supports, encouragement, and mentorship.

I look forward to that once a month, you know what I mean? I'm not happy that I'm on probation, but I look forward to coming to see [my PO], you know, letting [them] know my accomplishments, you know, letting [them] know how good I feel about myself, you know what I mean?

(Interview 1)

PMI-F admitted that he was more aware, motivated, and was making better pro-social and legal decisions; he credited being on probation for this change:

Q: What are some of the highs and the lows of being on probation? So, for example, what are some of the benefits you get out of—you've already kind of talked a little bit about that, but what are some of the things that are like good about being on probation, if I can even say good? What are some of the things that are not so good?

PMI-F: Well, it keeps you on your toes. It keeps you motivated to do something. You know, you can't slack off or you're going—you're getting locked up. And some of the lows are like the whole, you know, you got to stay on your Ps and Qs. You can't slip up.

(Interview 1)

Preventing slacking off and slipping up for this PMI meant following the rules of the law in order to avoid more jail time, which was reinforced through the behavioral conditioning that probation offered him.

Some of the data points toward a trend where the specialized services that these PMIs are receiving from their probation officers, who are in most cases overseers of their treatment and recovery, were not only comprehensively effective, but were also perceived by most of the PMIs as needed for behavioral change (i.e., there is an increased level of buy-in about treatment adherence). This perception of the importance of mentorship and role modeling that POs provide is reflected in Theme 2 and will be discussed in the following sections.

Theme 2: PMIs' Relationships with and Perceptions of POs

The second theme that emerged from the PMI interview data pertains to the ways that PMIs perceived the impact of their PO on their lives—specifically, the value of having their probation officer as a source of support, as an ally, and as a mentor as they navigated the mandates of treatment and rehabilitation. Although that "cheerleading" role was important to them, they acknowledged that to be successful in treatment, rehabilitation, and in their daily navigation of probation and the wider community, they had to adhere to the prescribed mandates set by their POs, which were ultimately governed by the programmatic and institutional ideologies and foundations of the probation system as a whole. These ancillary themes will be the focus of the next sets of findings.

Ancillary Theme 2a: PO Perceived as a Mentor

"I mean [they are] a probation officer, but they do look at you more or less like they can be—you can use them almost as a mentor."

(PMI-A, Interview 1)

All of the PMIs spoke directly to the benefits of interacting with a probation officer. As evidenced from data from both the first and second round of interviews, being on probation was a challenge for all of the PMIs. Nonetheless, these men professed that probation offered varied opportunities designed to help them right their wrongs and move forward in a more positive direction—and the PO was essential to that journey. Most of the PMIs described their PO as understanding and supportive in facilitating all essential aspects of probation, including mental health/substance abuse rehabilitation, as well as navigating the maze of services and opportunities in the local community. PMI-B, in particular, voiced the general consensus among the six interviewees.

> Everybody is fallible. Everybody is human. So not that they expect everybody to make mistakes, but they expect you to man up when you make those mistakes. And, you know, just do what you're supposed to do. Just—I don't want to say normal, but, you know, be productive. [You should want] to achieve more, and they'll be there to support you and help you and guide you, you know. If you need to find a better job, they have outlets for you to do that. If you're looking for more housing, they have outlets for you to do that. You know, it's just like you got to completely 110% take advantage of all of the opportunities they're willing to give you. And you just do the right thing, and they'll hand it to you. You know, it's not complicated.
>
> (Interview 2)

PMI-C spoke to the value of having a PO who helps to facilitate a substance-free lifestyle, which involves having fun and being around like-minded individuals. He shared an experience when his PO came to visit him, unannounced, to check on his progress and wellbeing, which was clearly a pleasant surprise for him.

> And [they] came to see me at the house one time and I didn't expect [them] to come. It was a surprise … and I heard the doorbell ring and I heard somebody downstairs saying, "Is [my probationer] here?" And I looked down and it was [them], and I wasn't scared because I knew I'm doing what I've got to do. And I came down and I said, "How are you doing?" And I shook [their] hand.
>
> (Interview 1)

During our initial interview, one PMI stated that he felt he was becoming more compliant with his medication regimen (mandated by probation), and credits his PO for not "violating" him when he struggled. He described the added value of having a PO who was willing to be patient with him as he got back on track:

> I started taking my medication. Well, you know … [I was really down and] it was rough. It was rough. So, I guess, that opened [my PO's] eyes up that, you know, I need help. And [my PO] was going to violate me, and [my PO] didn't. You know, [my PO] kind of seen where I went with

it, and now [my PO] sees I'm on my medication, so [my PO] was happy. [They] told me today and last week, my urine samples are clean now.

Another PMI also voiced the benefits of being in compliance—not only with his medications and treatment, but also in terms of being in sync with other mandates established by this PO. He described the stressful experiences that continue to make life difficult (housing, prior heavy use of substances, and his family health issues), but seemed content that "now everything is like sitting in its place, so it was pretty good. I can't complain" (Interview 1).

Probationer C was particularly vocal about the benefits of interacting on a regular basis with his PO. The engaging language he used to describe the value of the interaction and relationship is a reflection of the importance of the relationship.

Q: What are some of the highs and the lows? What are some of the things that you can speak to? What are some of the benefits of being on probation and what are some of the not so good things?

PMI-C: The benefits? The good thing is I've got somebody looking over me and I've got something to strive forward to instead of not having somebody looking over me and, like, not having something to look up to. Like, my probation officer could be a mentor if you look at it that way. Like I look at it that way, too, or [my PO] could be my support network. Like I say that in group every time we've got group, we go around the room and we say what's our support networks, and I say my probation officer's my support network, my sober support team. [They are] my sober support team because, like, if I didn't have [them] to see every week, I won't have nobody else to talk to about what I'm going through throughout my week or my weekend.

Later, PMI-C used even stronger language to describe his PO—as his hero—and detailed the powerful role that his PO played in his life:

Q: Being your probation officer, what role does [your PO] have in your life? PMI-C: A hero.

Q: Okay. A hero. That's powerful. When I think about a hero, I think about somebody who has certain kind[s] of powers that they use to help people. Is that the way you're thinking about it?

PMI-C: Yep. [My PO is] doing for me what I can't do for myself, basically, just telling me, Man, just do the right thing and do what you've got to do and be honest and open-minded. That's it basically, and

I kept hearing that. When I [got bad] ... I kept telling myself, Man, I don't want to do this no more, man. I'm done, man. I'm done.

Another PMI also noted the supportive nature of his relationship with his PO:

[My PO] is a part of my support group, you know what I mean? I look forward to that once a month, you know what I mean? I'm not happy that I'm on probation, but I look forward to coming to see [my PO], you know, letting [them] know my accomplishments, you know, letting [them] know how good I feel about myself, you know what I mean? Because other than [them] and my therapist and my teachers, I don't have support[s] on the outside world.

While this section focused on the benefits that PMIs perceived in their relationships with POs, the next section will provide deeper insights into the kinds of impressions that PMIs have about their interactions with POs and about the relationship that has developed between PMIs and POs.

Ancillary Theme 2b: PO Perceived as an Ally

"My PO's been awesome. I mean I've been, to be honest, I should have been back in jail a long time ago. And [my PO has] given me a lot of chances."
(PMI Interview 1)

There is considerable evidence supporting the finding that the probationers interviewed for this study had positive impressions of their relationship and interactions with their specialty probation officers. One probationer viewed open communication as essential to ensuring that his interactions with his PO were productive. Given their life trajectories and the problems they experienced—which sent them spiraling toward deviant criminal behaviors, drug and alcohol abuse, and dependence and other comorbid problems (i.e., intimate partner violence and other relationship problems)—it was evident that their relationship with their POs may have been the first wholly supportive one in their lives. Indeed, based on their comments, their POs seemed to represent more than an authoritarian figure and became something akin to a caring parent or trusted caregiver.

One PMI underscored the importance of this relationship and the open and honest communication used in maintaining a good working relationship with the PO:

[A]s long as you know it's an open and honest communication, there really is no issue. If I have a problem, I can come to [my PO]. If [my

PO has] a problem [they come] to me, same with all my groups and my counselors. If there's ever an issue, you know, communication can solve 95% of anything. So as long as there's that open honest communication and like when I screwed up a while ago, I told [them], you know, I screwed up, you know, and as long as you're honest about it, the consequences aren't as severe you know.

(PMI-A, Interview 1)

Another PMI stressed the benefits of this support and having someone who watches over him and helps him to work toward a set of laudable goals:

The good thing is I've got somebody looking over me and I've got something to strive forward to instead of not having somebody looking over me and, like, not having something to look up to.

(PMI C – Interview 1)

Ancillary Theme 2c: POs' Perceived Support Based on Contingencies

"Yeah, it's not a stressful one. It's not a demanding one. It's just, "Hey, do what you're supposed to do."

(PMI-B, Interview 2)

Although the PMIs reported that they felt supported by their PO, there were relational and practical contingencies that the probation system imposed, which then influenced the interactions between the individual POs and PMIs. Evidence supports the idea that POs were supportive and encouraging—but always within system-imposed boundaries. PMI-B, while acknowledging positive interactions with his PO, emphasized that the requirements of probation drove his relationship with his PO. In short, compliance emerged as the key to a successful probation experience, which he described during this initial interview:

So like our interaction, it's, I don't want to downplay it, and be like, it's not—it's a friendly conversation with that line knowing that we're not friends, you know, what I mean? That's probably the best way I can put it. That's how we interact or how I kind of perceive it. It's like we can talk about anything, we can even joke a little bit, but when it comes down, when push comes to shove, [they are] in charge of me. [They] tell me what to do. You know, but as long as I do what I do, we can have that not like buddy-buddy, but we can have that more relaxed relationship. Where I go in, I talk, you know, I give [my PO] everything [they] need, and then I just go home. You know, this goes back to doing what you got to do. [It] determines how [they are] going to treat you.

(PMI-B, Interview 1)

Another participant also spoke of the comfortable nature of the relationship with his PO, but reiterated the notion that compliance remained one of the keys to maintaining that association:

It's not a stressful one. It's not a demanding one. It's just, "Hey, do what you're supposed to do. You know, you're going to come in, we're going to talk about just life and how you're progressing and what you need to work towards, and we'll go from there."

(PMI-B, Interview 2)

This same PMI reiterated the value of having a PO, even though the PO's expectations were demanding at times. He also spoke about the inherent challenges related to being on probation in a general sense, such as the constant monitoring and the implied stigma of being on probation. Nonetheless, he seemed to value the helpful assistance of his PO.

You know, people have this weird outlook on probation. Yeah, the name itself sucks. You know, like, I'm on probation. I have a probation officer. They can monitor anytime they want. They can come and do whatever they want. But, man, as long as you just stay right, they really are just there to help you. That's the bottom line.

(PMI-B, Interview 2)

PMI-D also confirmed the support gained and the quality of the interpersonal connection with his PO—and especially that he did not in any way feel demeaned by his PO.

My probation officer, [they] never judged me. [They] never looked at me as, you know, as a criminal. [They] always got to know me, you know. You know, [they] didn't get to, you know, [they] never, you know, like things could be written down, you know, like crimes that you committed. But that's never been the case with my probation officer. So [my PO has] always treated me fairly, you know.

And [they have] always given me equal opportunity. You know, just as if I wasn't on probation. You know what I mean? [They] never compared me, you know, or anything like that. So I mean I'm being treated as if I'm not on probation. I mean, [they do their] job, you know what I mean? But I mean like I'm not being treated like a criminal.

(PMI-D, Interview 2)

Much of the interview data supports the existence of a positive, yet professional, relationship between the PMIs in this study and their POs. Several PMIs also described "getting to know" their POs as less of a criminal justice professional who is motivated to lock people up, but instead as someone who genuinely cares about them and wants to help them turn their lives around. These six PMIs appeared to understand that treatments were mandated with good reason—to help them work toward better health and recovery—as stated by one PMI:

> It sucks because I was mandated to, but, you know, being there, I went there very closed minded, and, you know, shut off. And then when I took the time to actually open up, like, okay, let me see what this is really about, and then actually be like, okay, I don't want to say like I'm as bad as that guy. That is just wrong on a whole different level. But it's like, okay, here [are] my issues, here's what I need to work on, and then I can be a better person. And because I'm mandated [by my PO] to go there, it made me realize stuff that I didn't see and things that I need to fix, you know, that I never would have noticed without being told to go. You know, so it's been a blessing in disguise to me having to go and make myself better, so to speak. But, I mean, it's a really good thing, you know, because of it, I'm a happier person. You know, I can deal with relationships a lot healthier now. You know, I'm not the scumbag I used to be.
>
> (Interview 2)

It was clear, however, that the PMI–PO relationship was not equal in any sense of the word. POs were in charge and PMIs generally agreed that they had to do what they were told and be open and honest at all times. One PMI recalled his experiences:

> In the first probably a month or two or three, I probably was still using. But I [am] truthful to [my PO]. I tell [them] the truth, because that's the first main thing [they] told me: "Be truthful to me. Don't tell me a lie because if you tell me a lie and at [the] end, it's going to hurt you in the long run," so I just told [them] the truth because I didn't want to lie.

He further shared in the following exchange that his impressions of his PO has changed over the course of his probation sentence and altered his experience of the relationship:

Q: So looking at your relationship with your probation officer, what is that like? How was it really forming a relationship with [them]?

How was it initially over the course of the last few months that you've been working with [them]?

PMI-C: In the beginning it was rocky. I thought [my PO was] out to get me and like, oh, you just want me to go get locked up, but that was just my perception of [them], and I judged [my PO] before I even knew [them] well. But now I know [my PO is good], and I love [them] for who [they are] because I know [they are good] because I see it, and, like, I couldn't ask for a better probation officer.

Similarly, one PMI spoke about the support he received from his "tough" PO, and how the relationship had evolved to the point that the probationer understood the importance of taking charge of his recovery.

Well, if you ever met [my PO], [my PO's] tough. [My PO's] a tough cookie, so [my PO keeps] me on my toes. You know, and actually, [they] could have violated me, because I caught another charge, and [they] didn't. [They] just, you know, [they] let me see where I take it. It's getting good now, because [my PO] sees that I'm trying to do, but before like I used to walk in there with an attitude I really don't care. You know, [my PO] kind of seen where I went with it, and now [they] see I'm on my medication, so [they were] happy. My urine samples are clean now. Yeah, [my PO] was encouraging, but … wanted me to do it on my own, because that's what you got to do.

(Interview 1)

Other more structural contingencies impact the probation experience— including the physical infrastructure of the reporting-in process, which more than one PMI described as intimidating. Nonetheless, one PMI stated that his PO helped in making him feel comfortable by treating him in a humane manner and encouraging his success:

As far as like a personal thing, I mean it does seem intimidating at first because first time coming into the building, you walk in, you got the metal detectors, you got the security guards. Some people might perceive it like scary or something like that. But then you got to go, you check in, and you do all this. It's like, it seems like this really long, weird process, and really it all boils down to you stay good, they treat you good, and at the end of the day, they want to see you succeed. They want to see you not go back to jail. They'll give you a couple of chances as long as you're honest, you know. That's not saying they're okay [with] you being stupid, but like I said, they're understanding that circumstances do dictate dumb things you know. So, yeah, they want to see us succeed, they don't want a person in jail.

(Interview 1)

Conversely, not every probationer appeared to appreciate the contingencies of probation. PMI-F had a somewhat negative view of working with his PO and invested little in relationship building. Nonetheless, he did indicate that the structure of probation was useful in helping him to achieve some of his treatment and rehabilitation goals.

Negative. Like I said, just like the whole you're not free, you know, like aspect. You belong pretty much to [the] County, you know, but in a way to me that kind of helped me, you know, because it gave me structure, you know. I didn't have that. I just—I was wild, so. I can't say it was—it was negative at first, let's say at my approach to it, but it helped me.

(PMI-F, Interview 1)

Another probationer cited the stress and frustration of having to see and engage his probation officer:

For me, it's been kind of stressful. I mean coming here. I know I've put myself here and I can't blame anyone but myself. But I think it's a waste of time coming here [to see my PO].

(PMI-A, Interview 1)

Despite PMI-A's negativity, the body of evidence provided in the interviews supports the notion that for the most part PMIs understood that they had to follow specific directives in order to remain free of sanctions or re-incarceration. The next section focuses on the narratives that PMIs used to describe their probation sentences.

Theme 3: PMIs' Perceptions of Probation-Related Expectations

The third overarching theme that emerged from the interview data with the PMIs pertains to probation-related expectations—specifically, the challenges and benefits of being sentenced to probation, and the factors (i.e., mandates and expectations) that played a role in whether the PMIs viewed them positively or negatively. These will be described in the following section according to three sub-themes that resulted from both interview data and live observations between selected dyads of POs and PMIs.

Ancillary Theme 3a: Insights into the Value of Expectations and Conditioning

"A typical probation visit is I come into the office. I sit down. [My PO] asks me pretty much almost the same thing as mental health."

(PMI-A, Interview 1)

This section focuses on the impact of these reporting schedules and the types of probation activities that occur during sessions between a PO and the PMI. This data was obtained both from interviews and from the two live observations between selected dyads of PMIs and POs. All of the probationers interviewed for this study had regular weekly or biweekly reporting appointments with their probation officers and varying probation requirements. Overall, probationers reported that they typically had good experiences during these reporting appointments, as evidenced from the following exchange:

Q: Okay, so in terms of your reporting requirements ... So what happens typically in these sessions?

PMI-B: Like from beginning to end what happens? [My PO will] call me in. It'll be some brief chitchat just to see how it was going. We'll talk about sports or whatever, and then we'll talk about how group's going, how my treatments are going, if I've had police contact. You know, it's just pretty much just an everyday conversation just to make sure that you're staying on the straight and narrow. That I'm doing everything I need to do, that I'm meeting all my appointments, and getting the proper paperwork back to him from my counselors, so it's pretty routine.

The observations provided a secondary opportunity to clarify some of these themes. During one of the PO–PMI dyad observations the discussion seemed to become more therapeutic and interpersonally enriching as the session progressed.

The session started with the PO asking the PMI how his week has been and [the PO] also asked him about what he has been up to. The PMI provided a response indicating that he has been working a lot and that there were opportunities for him at work. The PO provided encouragement and support to the PMI and there were many opportunities for dialogue through the initial portions of the session.

(Second observation field notes)

In addition, there were more positive relational dynamics (e.g., using humor) during the second observation that provided the PMI with the opportunity to engage with the PO and in some ways contribute to assessing his own treatment goals. The PO asked about the PMI's mental health treatment: "What kind of goals are you working on there [in treatment]?" The PMI then verbally provided a list of the following goals: (a) being assertive, goal-oriented, and focused; (b) improving communication skills; (c) engaging in healthy behaviors; and (d) using positive self-talk. In response, the PO asked the PMI how he was going to achieve those goals, to which the PMI replied: (a) going to weekly treatment sessions; (b) having positive family interactions; (c) being assertive, but not aggressive, in relationships; and (c) being more consistent in his attitude and behavior.

There was a lot of dialogue and reflections during the second observed session between the PO and the PMI. The PO seemed very interested in the experiences of the PMI and asked a lot of insightful questions, such as how the PMI was applying skills in his family and relationships and the status of the PMI's chemical dependency treatment. There were lots of positive affirmations and supportive statements. This PO seemed quite personable and interpersonally skilled in using humor and facilitative questions, which enabled the PMI to talk openly about the many gains that he had made in his recovery and mental health. As excerpted from my field notes, there was a lot of "dialogue about relationships, lots of psycho-education and the interaction seemed to me as a non-hierarchical and very engaging session where the PO seemed very approachable and client-centered (Second observation field notes).

Ancillary Theme 3b: PMIs' Personal Constraints Impact Perceptions of Value of Probation Conditioning

> "If I'd like to leave the county, I'd have to ask permission from [my PO] and get a signed sheet saying that I can leave. I have a ... curfew. If I want to stay out later, I have to call and ask."
>
> (PMI-A, Interview 1)

There were a number of issues that PMIs perceived as being somewhat challenging, and which may have colored the way they viewed the probation experience. For example, the brevity of the appointments with probation officers seemed to be a drawback. In my observations, a session typically lasted for at most 15 minutes; in response, some PMIs complained about the stress of traveling to attend a five- to ten-minute appointment. Although there was a relatively healthy perspective about the need to attend these appointments, there were perceptions on the part of PMIs of being restricted, confined, and overly regulated by the brevity and lack of substance in these sessions with their POs. One PMI shared that,

I'll just reiterate and tell you, I mean, literally our appointments when I see [my PO] last about, not kidding, two minutes, and consist of: "Any changes?" Usually no. "You've done any drugs or alcohol?" No. "Okay, how about I see you then?" "Okay, bye." That's the extent of it every time, literally that long, so I'm just giving you the heads up.

(Interview 1)

Thus, the brevity of appointments was a definite negative. This probationer also disclosed that one of his mental health providers suggested making accommodations about sessions but that the PO did not comply (Interview 1). The PMI seemed disgruntled about the intensity of his reporting schedule with his PO:

PMI: when my depression is really, really, really bad and I don't function much. Between that and how cold like this winter has been, it's just not possible sometimes for me to get here (Interview 1).

Q: So how do your reporting requirements affect your daily, weekly, or monthly schedule, your routines, what you typically do? Or in what ways are those impacted?

PMI: The only real [negative impact has been] psychological. There's some physical impact, too. I mean, psychologically usually last several days before and after the appointment I would say.

Q: What's been helpful for you as a result of this, if anything?

PMI: The only positive experience that I can say is that it's good on occasion for someone to forcefully have to come in, like have to do home visits, because no one does that outside. But it probably benefits me because I know that I have to, you know, kind of eventually take care of it and take care of where I live and everything. So that can be beneficial in ways, but overall I'm going to have to say that everything's pretty much negative (Interview 1).

These admissions point to a level of ambiguity for this PMI as to the benefits of his probation conditioning.

In contrast, probationer C mentioned that he had learned to accommodate and appreciate the reporting expectations—that he benefited from more structure, as indicated from the following exchange:

Q: How would you kind of describe how that really impacts your daily schedule— having to be here on a weekly basis or your weekly schedule?

PMI-C: It hasn't been. Like in the beginning, because I didn't have nothing planned, but now it won't really impact me now, either. We only

> meet each other for like three or five minutes and then I'm gone because since I'm doing so good now, it's not like he's got to see me for all, like, 20 minutes. [My PO] sees me for five minutes and I'm gone, catch the bus, and I'm back at group because my group [is close to here].
>
> (Interview 1)

Despite the brevity of the sessions, PMI-C appeared to see the benefits of having to report on a regular basis because it gave him some structure and something to do with his time. His rehabilitation plan—although initially challenging to navigate—was viewed in a positive light. It must be stressed, however, that all PMIs were required to attend their regular PO appointments for routine check-ins about their progress (or lack thereof). So individual PMI-attitudes played a big role in how they viewed their mandated treatment and rehabilitation protocols.

Some observations confirmed what several PMIs reported about session brevity and the lack of substance in interviews and appointments. The dialogue between one particular PO and his PMI seemed to be more of a criminal justice data-generating session and less of a therapeutic checking in, conversation, or discussion. In the first observed session, the PO started off asking "How are you today?"

> The probationer provided a gesture and seemingly reserved response that he was okay. The probation officer checked in about changes in address from PMI and about new phone number, and the PMI provided an updated phone number that has changed since his last visit with his PO.
>
> (First observation field notes)

This exchange typified most sessions—an initial check-in followed by a range of questions designed to update the PMIs status, with the ensuing information then entered into a computer database. In one dyad observation, it was evident that the PO was using more law enforcement competencies to inquire into the experience of the PMIs—principally because the PMI was continuing to abuse substances.

This section underscored how PMIs perceived their reporting sanctions and expectations as being a mix of positives and negatives. The evidence from both interviews and observations validates that the value of probationary conditions were intricately connected to how they described their relationships and interactions with their individual POs—and in particular whether the PMI felt that he was more than just an entry into a criminal justice database.

Summary of Findings from PMIs

These narratives detail the challenges related to treatment and accountability for treatment, and more specifically how PMIs perceived the nature and quality of their interactions and relationships with their probation officers. In summary, all the PMIs understood the role of POs as being professional helpers/enforcers tasked to implement the mandates set up by the justice system. They alluded to a powerfully hierarchical system of accountability, which they understood was meant to ensure public safety and guide the treatment and rehabilitation of individual probationers. Although some of the PMIs reported that they might have initially challenged or disregarded the authority and expertise of their POs, they ultimately worked towards compliance.

The findings obtained from interviews and observations provide a snapshot of the experience of probationers with particular probation officers. Without exception, the PMIs acknowledged the positive role that these probation officers served in their lives, using descriptors such as "a support system," "mentor," and "hero." There is strong evidence that PMIs benefited from the behavioral methods used by POs to manage and intervene using reinforcements, contingencies, and behavioral control techniques—including the threat of punishment. Evidence shows a relatively positive response to these strategies; they seemed to genuinely believe that the interventions worked and were implemented for their own good.

The impact of probationary mandates, however, must ultimately be measured in outcomes. Probationers were candid that they struggled with substance abuse, resulting in part from their mental health issues. However, all the PMIs in this study adhered to treatment based on a realization that their co-occurring problems could only be resolved through intensive, regular meetings with their POs, coupled with individualized mental health and group-based substance abuse counseling in local-area community mental health clinics.

To some extent PMIs have been socialized and conditioned to respond positively to the directives of their POs and to adhere to these expectations without questioning—at least they did not question openly during interviews or in meetings with their POs. This is both a benefit and consequence of participation in the criminal justice system. The relatively rigid structure helps to contain discussions and keep public safety as the guiding ideology. The structure serves as a way to control the behaviors and, in some cases, the attitudes of the probationer and the offender. However, the main drawback of these mandated expectations is that they may hinder (or even prevent) long-term change due to the fact that the PMI's independent decision-making capabilities are limited to a certain degree.

The next chapter focuses on results from the semi-structured interviews with POs. Their perspectives detail the work of POs in executing the mandates of the courts, which provides another aspect of the challenging task of helping their PMIs to stay healthy in the community and out of jails and prison for the long term.

4   POs' Demographics

Demographic data was obtained from the six probation officers who took part in this investigation. The ethnic breakdown of the POs included one African American and five Caucasians. The academic background of these POs was diverse and covered a wide range of disciplines. All of the officers had at least a bachelor's degree and three PO-respondents had attained a postgraduate degree at the time of this investigation. The work experience as a probation officer among this cohort, in this particular setting, ranged from a PO with just over two years of experience to one PO having worked for over ten years as a county PO. The POs in this study worked in a variety of specialty mental health and substance abuse treatment tracks—as opposed to supervising more traditional probation caseloads. Their work required particular interventions in these specialty areas and these responsibilities will be discussed in the findings. The results gained from multiple data-collection strategies will be the focus of the next section, with particular emphasis on the narratives that PMIs and POs used to describe their probation experiences, including the practices used by POs to help PMIs manage their lives. Although diverse, these narratives contain common threads that informed this study's findings.

Results from Interviews with Probation Officers

Although the primary focus of this investigation is understanding the diverse probationary experiences of PMIs, knowing the perceptions and perspectives of the POs who work with these probationers provides more depth and richness about this topic. As with the PMIs' data provided above, initial coding schemes were generated after a careful review and synthesis of the transcripts from the interviews with POs. The codes generated from the interview transcripts with the POs include the following:

1   POs' perceptions about managing caseloads.
2   POs' perceptions about engaging PMIs with comorbid needs.

3 POs' perceptions about doing probation: the work of rehabilitating and treating probationers.
4 POs' perceptions about personal and professional experience with mental illness.
5 POs' perceptions about their relative positioning in their specialties through their academic and work experience/professional development.
6 POs' perceptions of their relationship with PMIs.
7 POs' perceptions about systemic mandates.
8 POs' perceptions about measuring PMIs' and their successes.
9 POs' perceptions about working through ambiguities.

The following principal themes and ancillary themes emerged from the evidence provided from the interviews with the probation officers, which is also summarized in Figure 4.1.

1 POs preparation as professional helpers and interventionists:

   a   Education.
   b   Training and professional development.
   c   Professional and personal experience with mental illness.

2 Challenges and aspects of specialty probation work:

   a   Caseload management.
   b   Working with PMIs' non-compliance.
   c   Interpersonal nature of probation work.
   d   Relationship with PMIs as intervention.
   e   Using community relationships.

3 Specialty probation as both law enforcement and clinical issue management:

   a   Using law enforcement and supportive clinical toolkits.
   b   Working on the social work and law enforcement continuum.

Theme 1: POs Preparing as Professional Helpers and Interventionists

The themes that will be discussed in this section target the preparatory competencies and ongoing training and professional development in which the POs engage. In addition, their *in vivo* personal and professional experiences with mental illness inform their work and impact the types of interventions they choose to utilize. The initial ancillary theme and findings are focused

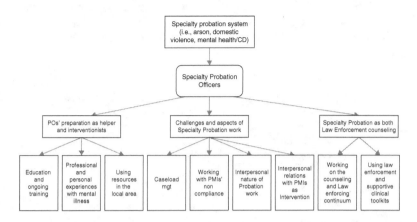

Figure 4.1 Thematic representation of POs work in relation to PMIs experiences.

on the educational background of the POs, which they agreed impacted their work as probation officers.

Ancillary Theme 1a: Importance of Education

> *"But at the time here in [this] county, it also required not only at least a four-year bachelor degree but also two years' experience in counseling, case management."*

(PO-B, Interview 1)

The POs evidenced diverse educational experiences, professional orientations (methods of supervising), and varied levels of expertise and experiences that informed their supervision of probation-sentenced offenders. All of the POs possessed, at a minimum, a bachelor's degree from a U.S. college or university in a social science or related field of study. Three of the probation officers had master's degrees with some including training in mental health. One PO mentioned about having a strong interest in probation work during college and, as a result, chose the appropriate coursework—a bachelor's degree track that provided the preparation for this position. Another PO originally intended to work in law enforcement, but had limited knowledge of the field of probation. This PO reported:

> I wasn't really sure, but that's where my heart was. Yeah. That's what I wanted to do, law enforcement, but like I knew nothing about probation when I was in college. Those didn't even really occur to me. And I just knew I kind of wanted to do law enforcement, but I wasn't sure if I could do it.

(PO, Interview 1)

One PO mentioned that a close acquaintance's work experience in criminal justice facilitated career interests in wanting to become a probation officer. In addition to their academic preparation, all of the POs reported that they had, and continued to engage in, required trainings sponsored by the Department of Probation. They also took part in professional development/continuing education opportunities intended to enhance their specialty service knowledge and expertise, which is detailed in the following section.

Ancillary Theme 1b: Importance of Training and Professional Development

> *"I know those opportunities are still there for us to go to different conferences and things that the community's putting on. And we do have some in-house training, too."*

(PO-E, Interview 1)

To remain proficient, POs have to engage in periodic mandatory training opportunities; additionally, they can also take part in other professional development opportunities based on personal interests and the nature of their specialty work. For example, officers who carry firearms have to complete 21 hours of peace officer training every year to retain their status as a peace officer. Another officer mentioned training on critical emotional response teams to further enhance skills and repertoires with PMIs.

Such training opportunities are particularly helpful in deepening their effectiveness and knowledge of community resources, which is critical for their work with PMIs. One PO, specifically, mentioned that there are added values to attending trainings that inform the work of a PO:

> We have trainings all the time, you know, because there [are] lot of things, including like DHS [Department of Human Services]. So we have trainings that come up for those. I like to take advantage so I learn more about those agencies. And then there's of course agencies I know more about, but who [I] don't always have interaction with. So if we have opportunities to go to training—[I go to] kind of know more about it and know how to assist them is helpful.

(PO-D, Interview 1)

Other professional development and continuing education opportunities offered POs a more specialized orientation to their work, which they considered important in helping them work more effectively with PMIs. For instance, one PO shared that professional experience and expertise in the mental health field helped facilitate a better understanding of the settings and referrals into which PMIs are sent as a condition of their probation sentence. This PO also noted that prior experience with co-occurring disorders treatment tracks provided an added level of expertise in the work as a PO.

Several POs mentioned other specific professional work experiences that later enhanced their role as specialty probation officers. One PO's earlier contact and interactions with other types of offenders facilitated the PO's interest in the position prior to the decision to take the qualifying exams. This PO's experience in a different context informed the work of understanding the breadth of needs that PMIs have. A particular PO shared that having some crisis-intervention background from the community mental health center helped to facilitate the transition into working with individuals with Mentally-Ill, Chemically-Addicted (MICA) issues. This PO described trainings and professional experiences that are enhanced by outreach, knowledge of psycho pharmaceuticals, and experience working with and learning from psychiatrists' assessment and evaluative competencies. Other experiences included working at a pre-trial diversion program and on a Driving While Intoxicated (DWI) offender caseload.

These varied academic, work-related, and professional development opportunities enhanced these POs' individual specialties and informed the ways that they interacted with their PMIs. One statement from an initial session with PO-A confirms the level of understanding of mental illness and recovery that is evident with this group. This deepened understanding was described as being really helpful for the position and offered a multi-perspectival understanding of how to meet the needs of probationers. One PO stated:

> Or just different nuances between, you know, making a referral to a drug treatment court versus mental health court. You know, that's kind of a fine [line]—you know, I have a pretty good idea about, and a lot of people will just say, oh they have a diagnosis in the past of depression. So, you know, and the person's using and using and using and bombing out [of] substance abuse treatment and then bombing out at mental health treatment. The instinct for, I think, a lot of the general supervision officers if they don't have the experience of treatment courts would just [be] let's put it in, you know, send it to mental health court. But I think the experience that I have is now I know that, you know, the access to personality disorders and the drug seeking behaviors don't really, they don't bode well in mental health court and they're not working in that [realm].
> (PO, Interview 1)

All of the POs commented on their relative positioning on the law enforcement versus counseling/helping spectrum, with all agreeing that they straddled the two. To illustrate this concept, one PO spoke of the role of helper/

enforcer, and how trainings and backgrounds helped with solidifying a professional identity:

> I think I'm somewhere near the middle. Maybe a little closer to the law enforcement side, but definitely still very much the [counseling] work side of it. Just because of my background. Because of the, you know, the degrees and experience and having to be the therapist, the counselor.
>
> (PO, Interview 1)

While it is important to note that the various PO specializations were mainly based on the mental health and chemical dependency needs of probationers, other POs were armed with specialty tools—such as working with arson-perpetrators, PMIs charged with domestic violence, and DWI felony offenders. POs valued their specializations and seemed passionate about their ability to intervene in the lives of their probationers and help them achieve a healthier life balance.

Ancillary Theme 1c: Importance of Professional and Personal Experience with Mental Illness

> *"That it's an illness like any other illness, and left untreated, it's going to get worse. That's it. If left untreated, it's going to get worse."*
>
> (PO-B, Interview 1)

A PO's professional knowledge of, and experience with, people with mental illness proved to be essential in how they thought about their probationers and how they conceptualized the nature of mental illness and how it might be treated. One PO with experience in mental health counseling, talked about the benefit of having diversified opportunities that informed and prepared POs for probation work:

> And then there was crisis intervention ... that's just a tremendous aspect of this job. And so that probably, of all my other jobs, prepared me the most for this job.
>
> (PO, Interview 1)

One PO shared about having an understanding of the biological etiology of mental illness, and having knowledge of the acute-versus-chronic presentation of different types of mental illness. Specifically, this PO spoke to me about the DSM-IV-TR conceptualizations of Axis I and Axis II disorders. Another PO noted the importance of being well informed about mental illness, which enhanced the capacity and ability to understand the underlying psychosocial issues that result from an individual's mental health condition. PO-C was adamant that a PMI's

> mental health issue is a big, I think, a big component of being on proba-
> tion. I think quite frankly people's financial stress, family issues, domes-
> tic violence, a lot of them [are] related to mental health issues. And also
> it's because this culture is more open than where you came from or where
> I came from about mental illness, but also it's tough. People don't want
> to say a lot about it. So it is a kind of hidden time bomb that is ticking.
> So yeah, mental health is a big factor.
>
> (Interview 1)

Similarly, PO-D indicated that it pays to understand the context and precipi-
tators of mental illness:

> I guess that it does make me understand more that they—like anyone
> you meet on the street, the reason [PMIs] might be acting a certain way
> [is] because they have these mental health issues that are going on in the
> background and you just don't know about them, you know. You know,
> like I have a client that gets very angry, but you know that [they have
> suffered abuse] in the past. And that is [the client's] defense mechanism
> to deal with people because [they feel] vulnerable, because of the abuse.
> So it helps you to understand that you know you meet some random per-
> son on the street and they're being angry, it's probably because they got
> something else going on, you know.
>
> (Interview 1)

In short, this professionalized understanding of mental illness facilitated an
increased emotional connectedness with the PMI and allowed this and all
other POs to be more empathetic and caring as professionals. Empathy, for
PO-D, was central to working with PMI's:

> I think I've been doing it long enough—I understand what some of them
> [are experiencing], you know, if they're hearing voices or I can under-
> stand that that's going to be really scary for them, you know. So I can try
> to, you know, [I] empathize with what they're feeling and, you know, try
> to come up with ways to deal with it.
>
> (PO-D, Interview 1)

Specialty probation officers also spoke about the importance of tolerance in
working with PMIs. Their clinical knowledge of mental illness made them
more aware of the amount of time and resources it takes to facilitate long-lasting

change, as indicated by PO-B: "It would be naive to think that you could take a lifetime of problems and change them in a month, you know, or even a year" (Interview 1). PO-F talked about the challenge of mental illness in terms of the added problem of substance abuse: "A lot of [PMIs] are [chemically-] dependent because they are treating their mental health ... with their drug ... I think they are kind of ... a lot of them go hand-in-hand" (Interview 1).

Some of the POs revealed their personal experiences with mental illness, which they indicated enhanced their understanding of the many challenges that PMIs have. They spoke of personal experiences with depression, and/or having family members, neighbors, and close friends with varied mental health issues. This personal knowledge of mental illness in all cases eliminated the naïveté they once had about the ravages of mental illness. One PO asserted that it motivated them to seek more education about mental illness, and enabled further work with this population of probationers, and helped to work on developing more supportive relationships with PMIs. PO-F underscored the importance of ongoing professional development in mental health as a key to building successful relationships with PMI's:

> I mean the best thing that I've learned is that I have to educate myself, so if somebody comes in with a mental illness and I'm reading—you know we get the PSI's [Pre Sentence Investigation], so it tells me. As long as I present in a way that is calming for them, I feel like I have had really good luck with developing a relationship with them. As long as I know what their triggers are and what they're—you know, especially someone with like PTSD or with—you know, as long as I know and I speak calmly and they're—it usually works out, you know, that I develop a good relationship with those clients—especially if they're in treatment.
>
> (PO-F, Interview 1)

The professional, and sometimes personal, experiences of these POs with mental illness augmented their understanding of the challenges that PMIs experienced. Such knowledge seemed to increase their levels of empathy and tolerance; most importantly, it provided a clearer lens for working with probationers with mental illness in ways that might increase successful outcomes. The second major theme that emerged from interviews and observational data addresses the challenges of specialty probation work, which is detailed in the next section.

Theme 2: Challenges and Aspects of Specialty Probation Work

Specialty probation work is qualitatively and quantitatively different from more traditional probationer supervision (i.e., working with general criminal justice caseloads). Simply put, the addition of mental illness adds a significant level of complexity to the probationary equation. Consider the challenge of ensuring probation compliance, structuring treatment options, and providing community resources (e.g., housing and employment) for a person who is grappling with a legacy of mental illness. These various challenges are grouped into five ancillary themes: caseload management, non- compliance, interpersonal relations, relationship with PMIs as intervention, and using community relationships.

Ancillary Theme 2a: Caseload management

"Yes, that's pretty much my caseload is the people who are struggling who are really the time consuming probationers that—because I have a reduced caseload in order for me to work in, obviously, the mentally ill, chemically-addicted caseload."

(PO-A, Interview 1)

The interviews with the POs revealed the types of cases and the nature of needs and presenting issues among the PMIs. The POs described their specialized caseloads as being relatively "small," ranging between 50 to close to 100 probationers. Given the added clinical component, however, the caseloads tend to be more challenging compared to the general probationer population. Probation officers supervised and were actively engaged with PMIs, who were described as having comorbid mental illnesses, substance abuse, and other significant psychosocial challenges, which were intricately connected to the rehabilitation and treatment services being offered in this agency.

In their work with MICA PMIs, POs were routinely engaged in the mental health and chemical dependency treatment progress of their client, which involved monitoring the requirements of psychopharmacology treatment. Another PO works specifically with the DWI-sentenced probationers, while other caseloads included a focus on probationers with domestic violence issues and again other specialized needs that the probation department aggregates for these specialty POs. One of the POs mentioned during the initial interview that some probationers are just "outright bad decision maker[s] [and that] these offenders are alcoholics [who] even with [threat of] state prison hanging over their heads [still engage in behavior that is] very difficult for them to give up" (PO-A, Interview 1). Additional evidence below supports this claim about the varied types of clinical issues that POs have to manage in their specialized assignments with probationers. Probation Officer A stated:

[My probationers all] have both chemical dependency and mental health treatment providers involved in their case, so they're just a little bit more attention seeking. I have a specialized caseload. They are referred to me by the general supervision or at the pre-sentence investigation stage, and they have to have both a[n] Axis I diagnosis and have substance abuse histories.

(PO-A, Interview 1)

Underscoring what is at stake in the management of probationers receiving specialized probation assignments, PO-F spoke about the risk that PMI-clients pose to the community:

A problem, yeah. They're a risk to the community because they're not being honest. They're driving, they're drinking. They're more of a risk I think sometimes than like gang kids that are coming in and at least being honest with me about what they're doing.

(PO-F, Interview 1)

PO-A, in speaking about management of PMI caseloads, stated during the initial interview that daily management of issues takes up a lot of the daily resources that are available, including time and other assets:

[I] have a lot of different people that [I'm] really trying to work with and, you know, because that's a lot of you[r] day is, I have about easily six people right now in crisis.

The nature of the crisis, as described above, is particularly personal and different for each probationer. PO-A described a particularly challenging domestic violence issue for one of the probationer-clients in their caseload, whose drug and alcohol needs were exacerbated by the individual's mental health challenges.

The POs concurred that frustration is a standard component of supervising PMIs with comorbid needs—largely due to the self-destructive choices and behaviors that many of their probationers engage in. These behaviors are often detrimental to the multi-tiered recovery, treatment adherence, and rehabilitation needs of probationers.

What I find to be the biggest challenge is the frustration of self-destruction. Folks that otherwise look like they are doing quite well and succeeding on paper, and it takes but a day for that all to implode, you know. Someone can go from, they're, you know, they're working towards higher education, they're working, they've achieved treatment goals, you know. You know, they're doing the right thing, and then next thing you know they're going out and getting rearrested, you know. I mean, it happens and that frustration is the most difficult that I find of the job.

(PO-B, Interview 1)

POs often talked about bringing treatment providers on board to help with crisis management, as well as using active treatment referrals to get the probationer into the right level of care. Evidence from some POs showed that the challenge is enormous and is often compounded by the self-destructive tendencies that a lot of PMIs have in terms of their pathological decision-making tendencies. One PO described an experience that represented a common challenge to the goals of abstinence and recovery for PMIs:

There was a domestic incident the other night … and—probation was called, the night team was called to the scene. [The probationer] blew a .065, so [they were] drinking. [The probationer] has a history of cocaine, heroin use, the whole nine yards.

(PO Interview 1)

Added to the substance use/abuse problem and the mental illness is the general challenge of just getting a clear picture of what's going on in their lives. In order to help, POs have to determine patterns of self-destructive behaviors that PMIs engage in on a regular basis—especially among their Seriously and Persistently Mentally Ill (SPMI) individuals. These clients end up taxing the entire mental health and medical systems because of the challenges of treatment and medication adherence.

Additionally, the theme of non-compliance in terms of both treatment and rehabilitation was an ever-present concern. POs employed a variety of strategies to work with non-compliance, which involved another skill set in comparison to POs who worked with non-PMIs, as detailed in the next section.

Ancillary Theme 2b: Working with PMIs' Non-Compliance

"Well, with my caseload, it's pretty inherent that they're usually not in compliance. They're people that are really struggling to stay compliant."
(PO-A, Interview 1)

The issue of non-compliance often determines a referral into specialized treatment protocols and increased mandates. A referral to a specialized caseload usually translates to added structure and helps to determine a more appropriate treatment and rehabilitation schedule for the probationer. The evidence also shows that POs usually provide multiple opportunities for probationers to re-engage in treatment and get back on track in the management of their health issues—even in the case of multiple non-compliance violations. Moreover, POs have at their disposal a number of options or tools for increasing the likelihood of treatment/probationary compliance. These usually involve the use of deterrents, depending on the type of clinical issue(s) that the PMI is working to overcome. For example, several POs mentioned the use of a court order as a tool to prevent long-term relapse—with alcohol use often being the target of the order. PO-B mentioned often telling a client that "well, no, it's not okay [to drink, even socially because there is] a court order. You know, and we can't, we don't get to pick and choose what court orders are enforced and what's not" (PO-B, Interview 1). Some situations required a higher level of intervention when a probationer "poses a risk to themselves or [to] the community, [then] court intervention is immediate" (PO-B, Interview 1).

The evidence shows that POs are well versed about the different treatment and referral options in the local community and they utilize that expertise and knowledge to engage their probationers. As PO-B indicated, "we have a lot of things, a lot of different programs at our disposal in this county. [This county] is rampant with services for chemical dependency and mental health and other problem areas" (Interview 1). In terms of assessing and facilitating compliance, one PO described the challenges:

> Well, with my caseload, they're usually not in compliance. They're people that are really struggling to stay compliant, and that's when someone would be referred from general supervision. But, so what I try to do instead of [and] prior to filing a violation, you know you're really working with the community agencies to try to get them, you know, going and get them back on track ... And if they're continuing to use or continuing to miss appointments or, you know, do whatever they're doing that's not in compliance. Eventually if they're just not responding, you do need to file a violation. Out of maybe four that I have to do, and this is [cumulative], this isn't something that's just overnight, my caseload. I put it off as long as possible. I mean, they really have to cycle through pretty much every [option].

> (Interview 1)

The evidence is clear that the POs in this study tended to utilize all of the available resources with the best interest of the probationer in mind prior to filing a violation. They worked diligently and hard through this process and exercised all accessible options before making this decision. Another PO mentioned the use of deterrents (threats of violation and re-incarceration) as a strategy for facilitating compliance:

Well, we have our deterrents. Even if somebody is looking like they're succeeding on paper and doing the right thing, I'm always using the deterrents. You know, I'm still doing the screening, I'm still, you know, supervising the way they should be supervised. I'm still going to be knocking on their door from time to time. The higher risk offenders are going to get that more often, but even the lower risk, they're still going to see me out there for deterrents. Now, sometimes you find those people, and they would, they look like they're doing fine. And let's say you walk into somebody's house, and they're intoxicated. I use that as an opportunity for an intervention to increase supervision, increase screening, make referrals for, to return to the treatment because most of these, you know—there's very few offenders that don't go in for treatment.

(PO, Interview 1)

POs also engage in treatment and rehabilitation-based supervision for PMIs through a system of accountability that puts the clinical needs of the PMI above all else—especially when the life of the PMI could be at stake.

And I tell them I know you're still using. I'm having you come in twice a week because I want to make sure you're alive. So—yeah, gives them something to do, gets them out of the house. So for people like that, you know you can't—I feel like jail is really the last option for them because—a lot of those cases, especially if they're a misdemeanor, they're going to go in for 45 days. They're going to come out, they're going to use, [and] they're going to die. We're going to—that's just going to recycle. They're going to be right back with us. So if jail is recommended, certainly [an option] like a bed-to-bed transfer with a halfway house placement [would be more effective], things like that. I've had really good luck with a lot of the residential centers here.

(PO, Interview 1)

Indeed, re-incarceration can have huge life-or-death implications for some probationers—and the POs know this. The recovering addict is at risk for reverting back to his substance of choice after a period of re-incarceration; thus, he or she would be better served through a referral to a structured and intensive chemical dependency treatment facility.

Some POs spoke about mandates—not as a punishment—but as a strategy to increase contact and ensure that the PMI stays alive, usually through a combination of criminal justice interventions and psychosocial approaches:

I have another client [who] started using cocaine again. Fine, I'm punishing myself too, but you need to come every week, because I obviously can't leave you by yourself. So, you know, and he did not engage in treatment after two attempts. Well, you have to go back to court. So that day I did a violation. And I only did a notice to appear because he reports as required, but the judge asked for a warrant. And I'm like, good, maybe it'll help him understand what's going on here. So sometimes it's necessary to be that law enforcement focus. You know, when they're not doing what you need them to do to better themselves, then maybe that's what they need.

(PO, Interview 1)

This same PO described a more personalized approach in which the value of seeking mental health services is used as a part of the intervention to encourage treatment adherence and engagement. In short, each PO had a significant level of variability in the ways that they approached the supervision of probationers. The various styles, techniques, and approaches—coupled with their educational background and professional skills—impact the choice of services and how they are rendered on behalf of the probationer. These individualized treatment and relational competencies are detailed in the next section.

Ancillary Theme 2c: Interpersonal Nature of Probation Work

"The rapport is important. The finding the hook, so to speak, what's in it for them? They need to buy into that."

(PO-B, Interview 1)

Multiple interviews with POs confirmed that case management and rehabilitation "really depends on the client and how they present … what the client does, what the client says, how they interact with me" (PO-D, Interview 1). They often spoke about the candid, highly interpersonal nature of their work in determining the specific issues that contributed to PMIs' poor psycho-emotional health and criminal behaviors. Additionally, they attempted to de-stigmatize mental illness by extolling the role of counseling—for anyone.

[PO-D tells] clients, you know, especially the ones that are not really ready to [fully examine their] mental health. I'll let them know, you know, sometimes you just need someone to talk to. So I think they all should give it a shot, you know. They might find that it's something they benefit from, that they like.

(Interview 1)

Although this PO recommended counseling as a voluntary choice, it was also clear that it might not be an option for some of the clientele:

Oh, you can't leave it up to them. This clientele, I feel many of them will not do it, will not get the help they need, unless you strong-arm them into it [a] little bit, you know. And many of them are just that mentally ill and they don't realize that. They think they're fine. They don't know that they need the help. So yeah, I'm very comfortable with [using that technique].

(PO-D, Interview 1)

Based on interviews and observations, it was clear that the work of specialty probation is individualized, interpersonal, and collaborative. It is individualized in the sense that POs often have to consider the particular needs that probationers have and work with them repeatedly and continuously to meet their challenges. Moreover, as noted earlier, their chemical dependence and mental health needs have to be handled simultaneously within a multi-layered system of community supports and criminal justice requirements. One size will not fit all in this milieu.

This work is intense, which is evident in the ways that POs describe their interpersonal commitments to their probationers. It involves recommending and implementing alternative approaches if tools and expertise that are being used are not effective. Essentially, the PO–PMI relationship is akin to the therapeutic relationship between a clinician and a client in that there are sets of clinical expectations and treatment planning processes that guide the professional interactions. And when interventions and techniques are not working, the PO must reevaluate the plan—typically in collaboration with the PMI and other treatment providers (i.e., mental health therapists, drug and alcohol treatment providers, case managers, judges, and other criminal justice entities). In short, the work of probation is individualized and there are lots "of external factors that may affect one [probationer] that doesn't affect another" (PO-B, Interview 1).

An important aspect of the interpersonal nature of probation work is that POs must be ever cognizant of their commitment to public safety. Thus, although they are committed to helping their probationer-client, services are fundamentally situated within the criminal justice system; thus, it can be challenging for POs to balance their dual roles as criminal justice professionals and concerned mental health advocates. An additional source of push–pull occurs at an individual level between the PO and the PMI, since there are constraints and challenges in any kind of goal-directed interpersonal exchange where each jockeys for power about the goals and potential decisions on how to accomplish goals.

Ancillary Theme 2d: Relationship with PMIs as Intervention

"I build rapport but keep it professional. There's no friendship there."

(PO-B, Interview 2)

POs described the quality of their relationship with PMIs as professional and usually very positive and engaging. Importantly, they typically spoke about their helping roles, as opposed to focusing on the potentially punitive aspect of their job. PO-D compared the PO–PMI relationship to a counselor–client connection. When asked to define the relationship with probationers, this PO indicated that "for the most part it's been pretty positive. It's been more along the lines of like a helping role as opposed to a punitive, you know? It's a lot more positive reinforcement rather than negative" (Interview 1). Nonetheless interview results were clear about the fundamental nature of the PO–PMI relationship, as evidenced in the following excerpt from this PO:

> But there also [have] been times when I have had to do the violations and had people do state prison time, things like that. So I definitely see it more, I don't want to say more as a positive force than traditional law enforcement or police but, you know, I mean even then more people view that as, you know, they're out to arrest people and that's it as opposed to, you know, we're here to try to help people. How do I treat the relationship? Well, we treat them like you would treat anybody else, you know. I still treat them as human beings like they should be treated, but professionally. You can't cross any boundaries, you know, because there might come a time where they might end up in jail, you know, all depending on their behavior.

PO-E had similar comments about the type of interactions shared with clients.

> I guess I need them to understand that we're not friends, but I'm going to be upfront with them and explain what we're doing. You know, I'm not going to hide, you know, what they need to do, you know. I'm going to be very upfront about this is what you need to do and if this doesn't get done then this happens. So, and I want them to feel comfortable enough with me to share things, you know, tell me what's going on in their lives.
> (Interview 2)

POs talked about the successes they had as a result of their ongoing work with PMIs. One critical and interesting note is that the evidence shows that successes are measured in distinctively different ways based on the kinds of specialties in which the POs engage. Certain mandates impacted the work that POs did on a regular basis and there were opportunities to discuss those directives and having to work at times with some ambiguity—especially with problem cases. One PO shared that one of the probationers "had absconded for a couple of months, you know, was really dodging, you know, calling with [illness], but keeping one toe in" (PO, Interview 1).

POs are still expected to adhere to the standards and rules of the state, such as having a certain number of contacts including face-to-face and home contacts. Moreover, there are monthly expectations that POs must complete and document. And when PMIs fall short of expectations or pose a risk to self or to members of the community, whatever interventions the PO employ must be fully documented—and in cases of non-compliance discussed with supervisors.

In carrying out their interpersonally based probation professions, PMIs must balance relational skills with the strict compliance regulations. While the work is for the most part individualized to the needs of the PMIs and the expertise of the PO, there are also many community resources and established relationships within the community that fuel collaboration in the care and rehabilitation of the probationer, as detailed in Theme 2e.

Ancillary Theme 2e: Using Community Relationships and Knowledge About Mental Illness

"Doing referrals and knowing what's available is a very important part of the job."

(PO-B, Interview 1)

The evidence confirms that knowledge of and expertise with local and regional community resources is very important in probation work. Similar to clinicians who work outside the criminal justice system, POs must be familiar with a wide range of expertise about community resources and how to navigate and gain access to these treatment options. One PO detailed both the opportunities and challenges involved in referral management and knowledge of resources:

It's really a benefit when we learn the things that are available in the community to help people. Because I'll be honest, I'm not even close to knowing them all. There are so many agencies that I just don't know about. I mean, I think if I did this job for 30 years, I would still not know all of them.

(Interview 1)

This excerpt speaks to importance of community resources in the PMIs' journey to wellness, as well as the daunting process of matching the resources(s) to the specialized needs of the PMI. In order to work effectively with a PMI, a specialty PO must understand how certain mental illnesses manifest themselves, and what interventions to employ. They must have a deeper understanding of mental illness in comparison to more traditional POs. One PO spoke to the challenges of working with PMIs and provided an example that supported the importance of a multi-perspectival approach to treatment and rehabilitation:

> You know, like I have a client that gets very angry, but you know that's [the PMI's] been hurt, like abused [and traumatized], in the past. And that is [the PMI's] defense mechanism to deal with people because [the PMI] feels vulnerable, because of the abuse. So it helps you to understand that you know you meet some random person on the street and they're being angry, it's probably because they got something else going on, you know. So maybe I won't … argue with them back, you know. I'll be like, okay, I'm sure we can figure this out.
>
> (Interview 1)

This more nuanced understanding of mental illness helped the PO formulate treatment needs, which includes designing and recommending/referring to the appropriate level of care and treatment agencies that would address the PMI's specific needs.

The POs also spoke about varied opportunities to empower the PMI, encourage their progress, and build and maintain relationships with treatment providers and other professional entities in the community. Although the responsibility for progress is shared between the PO and the PMI, the decision to get the best out of treatment is ultimately up to the PMI. Consequently, POs work diligently to engage these collateral contacts about the progress or lack of progress that PMIs are making:

> It's really up to them … They have to be the one that makes the appointments and go to them for treatment programs … After that point, you know, we'll call and make contact with their treatment providers, the counselors and therapists, fairly regularly to make sure that they're coming, how they're doing, and then encouraging them to keep going.
>
> (PO-D, Interview 1)

Specialty POs have to form and maintain professional relationships with treatment providers across a wide spectrum of treatment areas. Their liaisons with different entities in many cases are integral to the success of the PMI. PO-D mentioned interfacing with the coordinator of mental health courts regularly for updates, which positively influences advocacy for PMIs. This interagency collaboration was well established, collegial, and extended to fellow team members and other probation officers. PO-B mentioned that professional relationships with colleagues are also important, which in fact is perceived as helping to maintain quality interpersonal relationships with PMI-clients:

> I like being able to work with—I like my coworkers. I like, generally, I like the people that I work with. You know, I've never had that us against them mentality. It's we're working to achieve goals that are going to make the community best for everyone. I like that work. I enjoy seeing people be successful. I enjoy that everyday can bring something different.
>
> (Interview 1)

There were opportunities to maintain treatment-focused relationships through active participation in meetings and case consults. It was also important to know which professional to turn to when crises occurred, or when probationers had a particular need in a certain specialty area. Case-managers provide support for POs (and thus for PMIs) because they serve as a linkage to many resources in the community, such as helping with health and homecare referrals, setting up and expediting intakes, and facilitating evaluations through contacts with mental health and drug courts and other treatment providers in the community.

> There's a case manager from each of the agencies, [and local healthcare providers] you know, each of the case managers [are] kind of represent[ed], and it's fantastic because you have a go-to person any time. You know, you're not getting in touch with the substance abuse counselor. The case manager's right there. If you're having trouble getting the mental health counselor they're right— you know, they [are] available].
>
> (PO-A, Interview 1)

Another PO mentioned the value of using the same treatment providers, thereby establishing a work history with certain trusted agencies. As one PO noted, "There's a good network in [this city], between the court system and the different mental health agencies" (PO-A, Interview 1). A recurring theme pertaining to the types of interventions straddling law enforcement and counseling is the focus of the next section.

Theme 3: Specialty Probation as Both Law Enforcement and Clinical Issue Management

The academic background of the six POs in this study include the humanities, social and psychological sciences, and health management. However, their professional orientation as helpers and enforcers was principally impacted by ongoing professional development, daily work with PMIs, and active collaborations with providers. POs are empowered to fully utilize the full range of law enforcement and supportive clinical toolkits available to them as they engage the probationers on their specialty caseloads. The following narratives support the theme of PO as both a law enforcer and helper.

Ancillary Theme 3a: Using Law Enforcement and Supportive Clinical Toolkits

> *"Eventually if they're just not responding, you do need to file a violation. This is about getting support and getting you the help that you need."*
>
> (PO-A, Interview 1)

The findings in this section detail the specific competencies and skills (i.e., that are criminal justice and clinically based) that POs rely on when the relational and interpersonal skills fail to produce the desired outcomes in PMIs. Results from interviews and observations support the theme that probation officers use a variety of clinical skills, law enforcement competencies, and legal expertise to engage their probationers and help them transition into better health and towards some agreeable level of compliance.

Evidence shows that POs use court orders and violation of probation (VOPs), potential threats of incarceration, and jail/sanctions to encourage treatment compliance. Some POs talked about increasing the levels of structure and expectations: for example, having probationers report more often, using more urine and toxicology screens, and other approaches. Their knowledge of treatment programs in the local community and ability to navigate these systems on behalf of the probationer are supported by interviews and observations.

The specialty probation officer uses many of the same tools that traditional POs utilize, including home visits, office visits, and collateral contacts with providers, and checking in with family members when issues are related to home and family. One PO with years of experience in chemical dependency and mental health treatment talked about the availability and use of other tools:

> I've definitely either have always had or have developed the ability to be able to talk my way out of situations or into a situation, into getting somebody to actually say what's really going on. And, to me, I think that's probably the best tool that I do have. You know, I mean, we have pepper spray, handcuffs, batons, [and] things like that in our bullet proof vest. Things, you know—and then eventually guns and things like that, but, to me just the ability to talk to somebody is probably the best tool. And to show them that, yes, we may, walk up to your house wearing the vest with everything hanging out and, [you] may be scared, but it's, we're

not there to take you away. We're there to do a home visit or find out what's going on and see how we can help you.

(PO, Interview 1)

There are other tools that POs use in their work, particularly in the case of POs who supervise DWI offenders. For example, PO-B described the use of advanced technological tools, such as a device called "SCRAM monitoring bracelets that monitor for alcohol consumption 24 hours a day [during] home confinement."

However, findings show that establishing and maintaining rapport helps in the design and maintenance of goals and objectives—particularly when the supervision involves stringent and difficult decisions. This rapport represents an important tool that helps PMIs buy into the "opportunity that they've been afforded to make some positive change" (PO-B, Interview 1). Other behavior-related tools are also employed, which include both negative reinforcements (e.g., the loss of certain constitutional rights) and positive reinforcements. However, PO-B asserted that "positive reinforcements [have been shown] to work better than consequences … [such as] allowing travel out of the county or taking away a curfew, you know, things like that are always good tool[s] too" (Interview 1). In contrast, PO-E mentioned the value of using firm, but also flexible, consequences to increase compliance, including the threat of jail and sanctions. This PO admitted some reservations about negative reinforcement, that although it

> usually gets people to come around to what they need to do … negative reinforcement isn't the best, but if it can at least jumpstart somebody on the right track doing what they're supposed to. You know, that would [be helpful].
>
> (Interview 1)

Although they had to resort to punitive measures at times, POs typically indicated that they were not forcing treatment or rehabilitation, but instead were working to facilitate healthy behaviors and the wellbeing of the PMI.

> I'm not mandating anything so I try to tell them, you know, it's the judge mandating it, so either you want to listen to it. And I give people a lot of chances. I do, because if they're on probation, then, you know, they're placed on probation to try to change their behaviors.

Evidence shows that these specialty POs worked to engage PMIs to

> get [them] on board with [the PO] as a support system and seeing probation as a way out of jail and not just be [like] you're going to jail if you

don't do this. It's more like this is about getting support and getting you the help that you need.

(PO-A, Interview 1)

PO-C asserted mainly wanting to help PMI-clients, and didn't view them pejoratively. This PO extolled more humanistic values (i.e., empathy, respect/unconditional regard and genuineness) in his work with PMIs:

I always put myself—I reverse the position. If I were the probationer, how I'd like to be treated? I always ask, double-check myself how I will be treated. I like to be treated with respect no matter what I have done. I am [a] human being. I want to use this approach. That's one area. So that's really my first approach.

First and foremost, POs are beholden to criminal justice-related mandates that inform their work at every level (e.g., the nature and types of clinical interventions that they have at their disposal). They view their helping role as secondary. One probation officer detailed the mandates that are put into place—even as a PO. POs are required to adhere to state government standards, such as the number of probationer contacts expected in a certain period of time, and how to manage certain issues, as exemplified in the following exchange.

Q: But as a part of the criminal justice probation system, how does the system affect your work?

PO-F: There [are] certain mandates that are put into place, like how often we have to see people, what they measure out at according to the state in regards to what type of risk they are. The state mandates, you know, a person that's at [the] greatest risk, which would be someone who's probably been in and out of jail, multiple felonies, been in and out of prison, that we see them twice a week. And then there's people who only come out as being minimal or low risk that we're only supposed to see once a month. But that's probably the biggest mandate that determines how we do our job in relation to the probationer.

(Interview 2)

In addition to the required office visits for PMIs, POs talked about field and home visit requirements mandated by the state governing body. Depending on their client load, it was clearly challenging for them to manage their ongoing monitoring expectations. Consider this exchange with a PO:

You know, with some of the mandates you have to see certain people a certain number of times a month, you have to see them a certain number of times out in the field, whether it be at their house, at their treatment clinic, wherever. And a lot of times that's hard to do. For example, I know [one day] I had 35 people scheduled to see me, and then [another day the same week I had] another 30- something. So it can get tough. And then also trying to balance time to see, you know, certain people I have to see every month out in the field. Other people I have to see twice every three months. And it's just, to me it's hard to find that balance of making sure that I see people in their house without, you know, letting them know that I'm going to be there, because I don't like to do that just because, you know, then they can put up the good act if they know that I'm coming or if they know that something, you know, is going to happen. So, to me that's difficult, you know, following all the visits. To me, that's where it gets pretty difficult—just trying to find the time to try to meet everybody's needs. So it'll be interesting.

(PO, Interview 2)

Similarly, another PO described the multi-tiered challenges of meeting the obligations of the criminal justice system, but also spoke to the level of flexibility accorded in navigating the decision-making maze:

We got conditions here. We have to—we are responsible. The court, probation by itself is an agreement between the three: the court system, the clientele or the probationer, and us. So the obligation you have [is to] the system [to] tell me this is why this guy is here, or this person is here I should say, because of this. I have to abide by that. Have to be, yeah even though we are flexible—I am flexible, I feel, but at the same time, I have— the system [telling] me to [how to] handle [issues], to be responsible ... So I have responsibility and the system would give me this, yeah the system very much lay[s] out what I have to do as a probation officer, my profession. With the report, with the written report, the monthly or the six months report we have, and you see exactly when the person is not making payment, when the person is not making progress towards treatment program. Whether the person is working or not, whether this person is involved in any illegal activities. This is sometimes its specific, the system will give you specific direction, but at the same time it will allow you to be a little bit open and fit your own way of handling business. So I believe, quite frankly, that as a profession is there's a lot of leeway I can handle my job.

(PO-C, Interview 2)

The exchange, while reinforcing the well-defined structure of the probation system, also alludes to certain ambiguities and grey areas where the laws and standards are not entirely clear. PO-B spoke to this issue directly.

Q: Are there ambiguities? And if so how do you work to resolve the ambiguities between practice mandates and working to rehabilitate and/or provide care to your probationers?

PO-B: I don't think that the mandates are a barrier to providing services to the probationers to meet goals and achievements. I think that some very intelligent people in the state have done a lot of research to try to make things better. And the new supervision rule that began in [the] State no more than three years ago, that actually created less supervision for those lower-risks of offenders. That being said, it also created higher supervision for the greater risk offenders. You know, so I don't think there's any.

(Interview 2)

Another PO relied more directly on the standards and mandates of the courts in how expectations are implemented and structured for probationers–supervisees.

I try to stick with whatever the court has said. You know, if there's any sort of gray area, I'll either ask for clarification from the court, talk to my supervisor, whatever it is to try to figure out what specifically needs to be done.

(PO-E, Interview 2)

One PO describes gray areas related to PMI's bouncing in out of treatment. This particular PO underscores that orders and conditions mandate a violation if a probationer drops out of treatment, but that it may be counterintuitive to jail them if they have already set up their next appointment.

In summary, the data strongly suggests that specialty probation work exists along a continuum—with the counselor/helper role at one end and the criminal justice advocate at the other end. The excerpts also speak to the variety of clinical toolkits that the PO has at his/her disposal. The next and final section will focus on the orientation of the probation officer as both counselor and law enforcement professional.

Ancillary Theme 3b: Working on the Social Work and Law Enforcement continuum

"Certainly more towards the social worker continuum."

(PO-A, Interview 1)

The specialties of individual POs facilitated how they engaged their PMIs and the types of tools and expertise they used in treatment and rehabilitation. Most agreed, however, that they wore the hats of both counselor and law enforcement official. PO-D conceptualized this dual-hat orientation in describing roles as a specialty probation officer:

> I mean, we have some law enforcement aspects. But really we are [helpers and] social workers. We are case managers in addition to trying to keep [PMIs] law-abiding. We're trying to help them improve their life.
>
> (PO-D, Interview 1)

This same PO elaborated that each individual PMI's presenting problem and response to intervention will guide how the PO functions in the roles of counselor and officer of the law.

> All clients are different. I mean some of them just need you to be, this is how it is. You're going to do it or you're going to go to jail. You know? And others need a lot of help, you know. Where I know their appointment's going to take a long time. We're going to sit there and we're going to talk for half hour, you know. So I might many times swing to the social worker side of it … it really depends on the client and how they present. If they present as willing to try being honest, then I'm more willing to work with them and then I might be more on that social work side. But if they're presenting as very standoffish, they're not telling the truth, they don't want to be here and they don't want help, then it's, you know, you try to break that down, but you can't always. And then it's like, okay, well, do the things you have to do or you have to go back to court, you know. So to me, it depends a lot on the client how you're going to act to them or what you're going to do.
>
> (PO-D, Interview 1)

PO-E also spoke to probation work as being on a continuum between social work/counseling and law enforcement. While this PO clearly preferred the former, there were times when this PO had to resort to the latter: when non-compliance or a lack of motivation (or both) were evidenced.

> Yeah, I mean, typically I think we tend to go more towards the social work stuff, try get a link to everything, you know, any resources that they need. And any resources that the judge says they need, whether it's anger management, mental health treatment, [and] chemical dependency treatment, whatever. And then if they don't do that, that's when we have to go for the law enforcement thing and do a violation to have them go back in front of the judge for the judge to make the ultimate decision on what he wants done, or he or she wants done.
>
> (Interview 1)

Summary of Findings from POs

These narratives and added conceptualizations from the POs interviewed details the intricacies of probation work from the perspective of POs. What was discussed in the paragraphs above are the types of preparatory competencies, both academic- and training-based, that influence the ways that POs engage their PMIs and do their work. In addition there are components of the work (i.e., managing cases, working with non-compliance, and interpersonal issues) that must be constantly negotiated and re-negotiated based on the ways that PMIs present and how they respond to the varied social work-based and/or criminal justice-based interventions that were implemented. The tool-kits are inherently designed to facilitate compliance on the part of PMIs; and their use has become individualized as a result of the needs of the PMI and the expectations and mandates of the profession.

There are potential critiques and interpretations of the relevance, utility, and effectiveness of these compliance toolkits in that their use and overuse does contribute to the active behavioral and attitudinal conditioning that the PMIs are experiencing. And the larger expectation and mandate of the profession of probation by state regulatory systems reinforces the hierarchy, power, and domineering impact that criminal justice professionals like POs have relative to offenders, while also allowing some flexibility to engage PMIs in challenging, and stressful contexts, in the probation setting and in the community.

In summary, the results of the semi-structured interviews and observations paint a vivid picture of the complexity of probation work in treating and rehabilitating probationers with mental illness. It is a multi-tiered system that must balance legal mandates that are first and foremost designed to protect the public, while at the same time engaging needed community services to augment the likelihood of treatment success.

These narratives are particularly insightful as to the multiple roles that POs must assume, which are informed by their educational background, ongoing professional training opportunities, interactions with colleagues, and work with supervisees in a very challenging and demanding professional work context.

The final chapter will discuss these results in the light of a number of psychological perspectives. Chapter 5 will also review these findings as they relate to stigma. Implications in several areas are reviewed, limitations are noted, and recommendations for future research are suggested.

5   Discussion

Chapter Overview

This qualitative study was designed to investigate how PMIs experience probation in light of their interactions with their probation officers. The findings presented in Chapter 3 and 4, as evidenced from interview data and observations, revealed the complexity of the interpersonal relationships between PMIs and their probation officers within the context of both court-mandated requirements and varied community-based services.

Indeed, the PMIs who took part in this study enhanced and provided some insights about what is known about the structure, ideologies, and processes used in the criminal justice system—in this case, a specific county probation system. This chapter discusses these findings in light of the developmental and social-psychological implications of their experiences of PMIs. The research question, purpose of the study, and the subsequent design of the interview protocols were not about PMIs' developmental or cognitive processes while on probation. The majority of the thematic analyses of PMIs' narratives focused on their perceptions of the probationary rehabilitation and treatment experiences they are mandated to engage in. Analyses also included the perceptions PMIs have about their POs and about the probation system as a whole. The developmental changes in behaviors and attitudes that PMIs described and shared that they are motivated to attain, and the ideals they shared about having an opportunity to be renewed, psychologically, coupled with making differing and more positive choices, led to the conceptualizations and further discussion of these findings using developmental and social-psychological theories. This chapter also reviews and interprets the varied roles that POs play in helping to reorient the probationers with the goal of developing more healthy and pro-social behaviors.

This discussion of PMI–PO findings will be contextualized within two theoretical perspectives: (a) Erikson's (1968) Theory of Psychosocial Development, and (b) Giordano, Cernkovich, and Rudolph's (2002) Theory of Cognitive Transformation. These theoretical foundations will be used to interpret what these multi-tiered findings mean from both a human development perspective and a behavioral, motivational, and psychological perspective. This chapter will also discuss the potential role of stigma in these contextualized findings.

A principal goal of this study was to humanize probationers with mental illness by giving them a voice. In so doing, I wanted to challenge the often stigmatizing perceptions held by society that inmates, and more specifically probationers, are "less than complete human beings, unworthy, and less deserving than citizens who have not violated the law" (Allen, 1985, p. 67). This investigation fills a gap in the existing literature by presenting the insights and perspectives of PMIs regarding the probation processes used to address their rehabilitation and treatment experiences, while also providing a multi-layered view of this subject by incorporating the perspective of POs. I, as the researcher, sought to explore the PMIs' perceptions about how impactful the configuration and ideologies of probation are on their lives. I also wanted to consider the impact of the work of POs and their efforts to navigate the varied community structures available to them. I begin by describing the theoretical perspectives that informed the findings.

This chapter also addresses the issue of stigma in light of specific theoretical underpinnings: (a) social dominance, institutional, and structural stigma; and (b) symbolic interactionism and grounded theory. I include a detailed discussion of implications and recommendations for (a) PMIs and POs; (b) probation supervisors; and (c) professional counseling training programs. It concludes with the potential limitations of the study and recommendations for future research.

Developmental and Social-Psychological Perspectives that Informed the Findings

Giordano et al.'s (2002) Theory of Cognitive Transformation, coupled with Erikson's (1968) Theory of Psychosocial Development, provided a foundation for describing conceptually how the PMIs' experiences reflect existing developmental theory. I limited this discussion to just these two perspectives because of their relative fit and appropriateness to a theoretical exploration of the findings.

Cognitive Transformation

The Theory of Cognitive Transformation is useful for describing a PMI's professed journey in leaving behind prior criminal behavior and self-destructive behaviors. In describing Giordano's theory, Healy and O'Donnell (2008) noted the following: "cognitive transformation envisions desistance as an interaction between structural and agentic factors, but posits the individual as the key driver of change" (p. 26). In this perspective, the social and interpersonal experiences that the individual (i.e., the offender) has, helps to facilitate action towards change. And in order for desistance and change to occur, the offender must have the motivation to move forward on the continuum of change. In the case of these probationers interviewed in this study, there are evident extrinsic motivations (i.e., not going to jail or facing sanctions) that help create a hook for change, in addition to the efforts of their POs. It is also evident that the opportunities for reform, rehabilitation, and treatment are seen as meaningful engagements, from the perspective of the PMIs and the POs, and so there are the seeds for the renewals and many other opportunities (i.e., social benefits) that facilitate these increased motivations. Healy and O'Donnell (2008) also noted that "the eventual outcome of th[ese] process[es] [of change and motivation] is a transformation from a criminal to a non-criminal identity" (p. 26).

These themes of change and deepening motivation were resoundingly present in the narratives of the PMIs interviewed in this study, as evidenced by their stated motivation to desist from criminal activity and make pro-social and legally responsible decisions. The narratives detailed in Chapter 3 indicate that probationers valued the opportunities afforded by probation and, to varying degrees, viewed the conditioning that the system offered them as being essential to their intention to improve their situation.

Although it is impossible to state categorically that the six probationers who participated in this study have completely desisted from crime or will continue to practice the same pro-social behaviors on a long-term basis after finishing probation, the evidence supports the expectation that they will do so. Indeed, all six indicated that they valued the probation experience as a way to stay out of trouble and try to make the most of their specific probation requirements—although some admittedly found it difficult.

In reflecting on the findings, and thinking across all contexts in the criminal justice system, it is likely that adherence offers so many more opportunities than non-adherence. Adherence can come with systemically sanctioned privileges that reduce stress and obviate certain life choices intended to help the probationer. For the probationer to be successful in his probation experience, he has to listen to, follow the recommendations of, and willingly (or even unwillingly) participate as a consumer of services—whether he sees the efficacy of the interventions or not. This is a necessary condition of desistance in that there is a forced decision that the probationer must make to desist from criminal behaviors because the benefits of desisting far outweigh the potential gains from a lifestyle of crime and deviance—at least during the probationary period. The system expects absolute compliance that PMIs will behaviorally buy-in to these conditions and processes of probation; what happens beyond that point is out of the PO's control. They have accepted that to be a "successful" probationer, each must attempt to meet all expectations and adhere to socially constructed perceptions of the value of transformation, reformation, and rehabilitation. In short, they know their roles and have agreed to adhere to them.

However, as evidenced from this study, adhering to the mandates of probation was viewed as a source of rehabilitation and renewal—in large part and as a result of the interpersonal relationships PMIs shared with their probation officers, who provided that "framework for individual action that either constrains or facilitates change" (Healy & O'Donnell, 2008, p. 26). In general, PMIs expressed insights about their struggles and worked to address them through a variety of therapeutic and criminal justice mandates, such as chemical dependency, counseling, mental health interventions, medication-assisted treatments, GED classes, employment searches, and criminal justice interventions ultimately focused on freeing them from the criminal justice system and returning them to society as fully functioning members with a "non-criminal identity."

In repeated instances, PMIs described a conditioned motivation for self-transformation—about making better decisions, about wanting to make things better in their intimate and familial relationships, and about wanting to desist from criminal behaviors that would lead to serious consequences. They spoke about being more mindful of the people, places, and things in the social environment that once played a key role in their negative actions and criminal behaviors in order to avoid them. Without exception, these six men were more positive in their outlook and in seeking positive opportunities because of their exposure to the "hook for change" in the form of probation and their relationship with their PO (Giordano et al., 2002; Healy & O'Donnell, 2008, p. 26).

Whether the PMIs will ultimately be able to adhere to permanent change and embrace their non-criminal identity is beyond the scope of this investigation. As such, an extended longitudinal study would be useful for assessing the longer-term outcomes of probationary interventions. Nonetheless, everyone participating in this investigation (i.e., the PMI, the PO) seemed to believe in the efficacy of the interventions and expectations.

Erikson's Theory of Psychosocial Development

Erikson's (1968) Theory of Psychosocial Development provides another lens through which PMIs' narratives can be understood. The human life cycle, according to Erikson, involves eight distinct stages: *basic trust versus mistrust, autonomy versus shame and doubt, initiative versus guilt, industry versus inferiority, identity versus identity confusion, intimacy versus isolation, generativity versus stagnation*, and *ego identity versus despair*. As indicated by the duality of these stages, they correspond to a series of "crises" that are experienced as an individual matures from infancy through youth and ultimately into adulthood (Erikson, 1968; Munley, 1977). Erikson defined the term "crisis" as a "decisive or critical turning point, which is followed by either greater health and maturity or by increasing weakness" (Munley, 1977, p. 262). Erikson (1968) purported that an individual must ideally confront and resolve vulnerabilities in each stage before successfully transitioning to the next stage—although mastery of one level is not required for moving on to the next (Erikson, 1968; Munley, 1977).

As a child grows and matures, the sociocultural environment of the child also changes, whereby he or she "comes into contact with a widening radius of significant individuals and institutions" (Munley, 1977, p. 262). These changes are based on the "mutual interaction between [the] individual's development and society, the [sociocultural milieu] in which that the person lives and functions in" (Munley, 1977, p. 262). According to Erikson, the crisis of each developmental stage must be resolved in a timely manner to allow developmental progression through the natural age markers (i.e., the child in infancy must be able to trust his parents or caregivers in order to become an autonomous being). Failing to successfully complete a stage can undermine the person's ability to get through the subsequent stages, resulting in a reduced sense of self and ability to overcome challenges. In contrast, when an individual successfully manages and negotiates the task of a given stage, opportunities for strength and solidarity related to the personality are created, which makes a subsequent navigation to the next stage possible (Miller, 2002). Munley (1977) stated that "these basic attitudes theoretically contribute to an individual's psychosocial effectiveness and personality development" (p. 262), while the failure to develop a healthy ego identity will likely lead to difficulty in commitments (i.e., interpersonal and intrapersonal) isolation, and a range of problems in later life.

In another research addressing threats to developmental adjustment (i.e., crisis in the psychosocial theory), Maggs, Frome, Eccles, and Barber (1997) asserted that in the realm of adolescent risk behavior and young adult adjustment, "individuals who began the transition to young adulthood from a position of strength evidenced greater adjustment" (p. 114). They indicated that adolescents who were psychologically well adjusted had huge gains academically, and "tended to experience more success in occupational, relational, and health [including mental health] domains" (p. 114).

Conversely, Maggs et al. (1997) found that comorbid "alcohol use, illegal drug use, and antisocial behavior predicted an increased likelihood of being involved in [pathological behaviors] and in relationships characterized by psychological and physical negativity" (p. 114).

Evidence from the Maggs et al. study supports this relationship and the importance of Erikson's (1968) developmental stages. Each of the PMIs spoke of one or more psychosocial crises or issues in childhood that challenged their healthy development. Specifically, they discussed problems resulting from limited parental presence and support/guidance, such as their introduction to drug and alcohol use/abuse at critical developmental phases of pre-adolescence and mid-adolescence. They also pointed out that early introduction to criminal behavior and deviance significantly impaired their ability to cope and led to further mental health issues. As they matured, these issues negatively impacted their performance in school, their interpersonal relationships with supportive adults, their interactions with positive role models, and their ability to hold a job.

Pinpointing the particular stage(s) in Erikson's developmental model where problems began to arise for each of these PMIs is both difficult and beyond the realm of this investigation. However, a more general conceptualization of how this theoretical foundation underpins the findings discussed herein is worthwhile. It is probable that most, if not all, of the probationers interviewed in this study actually failed to successfully negotiate a number of different psychosocial stages. The PMIs discussed their early developmental challenges—including being raised in a tumultuous household with rampant drug and alcohol use and early exposure to criminality. As we can recall, Erikson's (1968) first developmental stage is *basic trust versus mistrust*, which occurs from infancy to about two years of age. During this stage children develop a sense of trust from caregivers who provide reliability, affection, and care. In the presence of such caregivers, the child learns to trust and develops a sense of security. In contrast, when this support is absent, the child develops an inherent mistrust of others and is at greater risk for depression. I would speculate that the PMIs in this study may have lacked the "favorable ratio of trust to mistrust" (Miller, 2002, p. 151), and that the balance was pathologically skewed toward mistrust, thereby leading to a lack of the "essential trustworthiness of others as well as a fundamental sense of one's own trustworthiness" (Erikson, 1968, p. 96). This developmental challenge may account for the lack of trust that was seen in how the PMIs initially perceived their POs. On many accounts, the PMIs shared that trusting and accommodating the requirements of their POs took an extended amount of time while under intense interpersonal circumstances.

Hypothetically, if PMIs had been able to successfully resolve this initial stage and gain a sense of mastery related to "getting and giving" (Miller, 2002, p. 152), it might have been easier to manage crises and challenges (i.e., to gain autonomy as opposed to experiencing shame and doubt). And indeed, trust was a common theme in our conversations. The PMIs specifically mentioned their growing capacity to trust their probation officers based on the perceptions of the healthy interactions that they have with them. In all cases, the establishment of trust involved a developmental progression during which they came to see their PO as a supporter, mentor, and ally. It must be noted, however, that it is possible that the orientation and philosophy of specialty probation officers enabled them to offer more specialized services in comparison to traditional POs, which may have reduced the relational differentials and created more opportunities for joint goal setting and interpersonal commitments—thereby enhancing the trust factor.

Another potential developmental challenge that the findings support pertains to Erikson's stage of *industry versus inferiority*. In this stage, the school-aged child (i.e., 5 to 11 years of age) asks the existential questions: How do I make it in this complicated world of people and things? Am I capable of making it in this world? In this stage, the child is exposed to new social and academic demands, such as making new friends, learning new material, engaging with more adults. With constructive and supportive feedback and social and academic successes, the child develops self-confidence, competence, and intrapersonal strengths. In contrast, in the absence of praise and success in activities, the child can develop feelings of inferiority.

This idea of agency/industry and inferiority resonated in the findings for the PMIs in this study, all of whom experienced difficulties in school, obtaining and maintaining gainful employment, and providing a source of sustenance for self and others. For example, several of the PMIs were attending GED classes, and out of the six PMIs interviewed, only one had been gainfully employed in the six months prior to data collection. Interestingly, many cited work and school as important components of their probation sentence—which supports Erikson's assertion that mastery of one stage was dependent on mastering the one before it. It is entirely possible that early challenges such as lack of resources, and scarcity of academic praise and support from important people (i.e., educators, educational systems, caregivers and other adults) resulted in feelings of inadequacy and weakness.

From a developmental perspective, there are implications that ill-fated trajectories in late childhood and middle-to-late adolescence impact opportunities for agentic behavior in young adulthood. The research of Dmitrieva, Monahan, Cauffman, and Steinberg (2012) asserted that "adolescence is marked by increases in psychosocial maturity that influenced improvements in temperance (the ability to curb impulsive and aggressive behavior), perspective (the ability to see things from multiple temporal and social vantage points), and responsibility (the ability to function autonomously)" (p. 1073). These researchers also stated that:

> There is significant variability in the degree and rate of development of psychosocial maturity across adolescence and young adulthood, with

some youth showing greater or faster gains and others exhibiting little or very slow growth in maturity over time ... The extant literature on the development of psychosocial maturity suggests that normative variations in social context may contribute to individual differences in the development of temperance, perspective, and responsibility.

(p. 1073)

Parents and other important early caregivers and smaller cultural systems (schools and sports) are tasked with helping youths develop appropriate maturational processes (i.e., identity development and search for prosocial independence) needed to gain certain competencies. Rules represent an important strategy for managing the explorative tendencies that youths at this developmental stage possess. Indeed, rule-setting corresponds to early preparation for engaging in society as law-abiding, fully functioning adults (Miller, 2002). However, their earlier inabilities to fully transcend the psychosocial stages (i.e., from birth to age three or four years old and potentially other stages) is suggested as one of the more important rationales for their involvement in the criminal justice system. These developmental and social-psychological perspectives can also potentially account for some of the mental health and substance use issues that PMIs were trying to resolve in their young adulthood phase of life (Miller, 2002). The issue, then, is that these PMIs appeared to be unable to or challenged to fully access the relational competencies that typically result from the presence of capable, nurturing, and supportive adults in early adulthood. They were also challenged by their lack of generativity, which then facilitated what developmental psychologists term self-absorption, self-indulgent behaviors, and a lack of sustained psychological growth (Miller, 2002) in the middle adulthood phase of life.

As detailed in Chapter 4, the POs in this study wore multiple hats in interacting with the PMIs: caretaker, support system, ally, mentor, and authority figure. One could argue, then, that the POs represented a type of parental or familial influence that the PMIs lacked during earlier and critical developmental stages. For all of the PMIs, being on probation represented a shared opportunity to gain some mastery over their lives from the wreckage wrought by juvenile drug and alcohol abuse and mental illness. In addition, the PMIs valued their POs' support and viewed it as a type of a restorative relationship that was reshaping their development in a positive way, as well as helping to build psychological growth through treatment and rehabilitation.

As mentioned above, findings suggest that the probation officers in this study served as developmental assets in the lives of these probationers. They worked to build and maintain the trust of their PMIs by using their interpersonal skills to encourage PMIs to engage in better treatment and healthier lifestyles. POs used their professional law enforcement authority, social work skills, and mentoring abilities to foster the rehabilitation and treatment of PMIs. Like any nurturing parent, they praised them when they were successful and challenged them in the face of potential regression and actual relapse. This guidance facilitated a positive treatment-seeking attitude on the part of PMIs and increased their desire to continue on the path toward sobriety, personal development, and recovery. In addition to a range of social work and law enforcement strategies at their fingertips, the POs also employed various clinical toolkits and interpersonal assets (i.e., empathy, building a therapeutic relationship, and offering support and structure within the relationship), all of which helped to facilitate this developmental progression toward goal achievement and improved quality of life for the probationers.

Viewed more critically, however, who is to say that the values the POs push and the opportunities they afford through these structures and mandates are in alignment with the sociocultural needs and psychological capacities that PMIs require for optimal development and progression through the life cycle? Erikson proposed his theory with middle-class, majority-cultured, and non-deviant groups in mind. As such, the varied experiences of the poor, deviant, and marginalized—not to mention those with a criminal history—are unlikely to support many of the developmental tasks involved in the social and emotional development of children and teenagers. Indeed, developmental challenges were prominent in these PMI narratives.

Nonetheless, while there are general developmental crises and events that are cross-cultural, other developmental situations are uniquely cultural and require relevant and culturally appropriate interpretations that align with the lived experiences of "others." These PMIs came from diverse ethnic, socioeconomic, and racial backgrounds, which makes applying a cookie-cutter approach to generalizing about appropriate developmental milestones somewhat risky.

The Specialty Nature of POs' Work

The findings presented herein have confirmed that probationers with mental illness present an added level of challenge for the criminal justice system—and specifically for the county probation system in which this study was conducted. Their concomitant problems of substance abuse, depression, homelessness, and employment challenges require specialized skills and strategies to help them progress and avoid future criminal activities. The specialty probation systems described in the introductory chapter and the evidence from interviews with POs confirmed that this particular probation system was relatively well-equipped to deal with the needs of PMIs. Although there is research (see Skeem & Louden, 2006) that alludes to the general inability of probation systems to adequately meet the unique needs of

PMIs due to interpersonal, strategic, and structural issues, such impediments were not evident in this county system. The specialty probation officers who took part in this study were all well-trained, experienced, and wholly directed at helping their clients via a range of practical and therapeutic approaches. Their efficacy, however, was highly dependent on their ability to form effective working relationships with the PMIs. As detailed in Chapter 4, PMIs generally used positive narratives to describe the overwhelmingly supportive roles that their POs play in their lives and recovery, and in helping them to sustain a better quality of life where their mental health issues are addressed and managed. Their collective reference to POs as allies, mentors, heroes, and a major source of sobriety support represents powerful descriptors that support efficacy of their efforts.

The various relational variables that manifested themselves during interviews and observations—such as the POs' perceived ability to empathize about issues related to the probationers' lives and experiences—served as evidence that this relationship extended beyond the confines of court-mandated interactions. Indeed, the interactions I witnessed assumed the form of a true therapeutic alliance, which is well described in the counseling literature and known to positively impact the effectiveness of treatment and rehabilitation outcomes (see DeLude, Mitchell, & Barber, 2012). POs stressed the importance of developing and maintaining supportive relationships with their PMIs as a component of treatment success; similarly, PMIs described many benefits of interacting with their POs on a "specialty basis" in comparison to prior experiences with other traditional criminal justice–oriented POs.

Both POs and PMIs perceived their professional interactions as being highly positive in that the PMIs benefited from interventions and POs gained satisfaction from knowing they were making a difference and facilitating the developmental progress of their clients. Although there were occasionally threats of PO-imposed sanctions as a component of their intervention strategy, the PMIs in this study did not feel that these types of techniques hindered trust or created challenges to the interpersonal exchange (see Kras, 2013)—especially later in the relationship once both parties got to know each other in a professional capacity. The values of this relationship-building is important to note, as the discussion now shifts to stigma and whether the practices of POs influence the widespread stigmatization of probationers with mental illness.

Stigma

Stigma is a negative reaction to a person (or persons) with a devalued identity (i.e., mental illness, criminality), which intentionally or unintentionally discredits the targeted person (Byrne, 2000; Goffman, 1963). Using perceived labels like "unpredictable, dangerous, and violent" to characterize individuals with severe mental illness in a society that so easily assigns labels can exacerbate the problem of mental illness by marginalizing or isolating those bearing the mark. All of the POs interviewed in this study described the challenges of working with probationers with mental health and psychosocial problems; in fact, they sometimes used language that could potentially be stigmatizing such as "alcoholic" and "psychotic." Nonetheless, I interpreted their language as more of a reflection of the difficulties of their work with individuals who are significantly challenged in terms of their mental health. The POs I interviewed had learned to accommodate the varied presentations of mental illness within the confines of the criminal justice system and the community. Hartwell (2004), in an attempt to avoid stigmatizing language, described offenders involved in the illicit drug industry (i.e., addicts, abusers, and dealers) as "suspect populations" (see also Beckett & Sasson, 2000). Rather than assign pejorative descriptors, he then defined suspect populations as individuals who "are composed of the disenfranchised poor who live in socially disorganized communities" (Hartwell, 2004, p. 85). Additionally, they are likely to present with limited skills and job prospects and with varied, but significant, disabilities. Hartwell added that they tend to be "alienated from the norms and expectations of opportunity in a capitalist society ... and are groups of individuals who are stigmatized" (2004, p. 85).

Stigma is nearly always attached to actions and behaviors that are non-normative and to the public's general intolerance for deviance. People with mental illness become further marginalized when they "become entangled with the criminal justice system. The inability of the marginalized to make rational decisions and risk/benefit calculations are compromised by their illness and addiction" (Hartwell, 2004, p. 85; see Beckett & Sasson, 2000), which further manifests the likelihood of stigmatization.

The data from this study (both PMI self-reported and from POs) indicated that PMIs were often challenged in their decision-making processes in terms of their drug and alcohol use. As stated by Hartwell (2004), their relatively recent and in some cases ongoing "involvement as consumers in the drug trade makes them vulnerable to formal forces of social control" (p. 85), which indeed is why they were available to take part in this investigation (i.e., studying perceptions and experiences while embedded in the challenges of navigating interpersonally conveyed mandates). Despite their three-pronged risk for stigma as probationers *and* individuals with mental illness *and* being deviant, the PMIs did not explicitly indicate that they felt or experienced any stigma from their interactions with their POs. Although the interactions I witnessed and the interview data I obtained could have been filtered or colored by virtue of the power differential between POs and probationers, there was no evidence of individual-level stigma in their interactions. To the contrary, data supports the notion of acceptance in this relationship in that PMIs expressed feeling supported and respected in their dyads. Nonetheless, in interpreting the interview data regarding stigmatization, I was mindful that what was spoken did not necessarily reflect what the participant chose to keep unspoken and unacknowledged. In general, however, their experiential narratives did not convey challenges related to stigma, which I had not anticipated given the disparities in power and influence in the relationships between POs and PMIs.

The stigma of deviance, criminality, and mental illness represents a potential triple-threat for the probationer. In the narratives obtained during this investigation, PMIs appeared to be complying with the mandates of the probation system and the larger criminal justice system: do what you are expected to do, do your time, stay in compliance, and be a good probationer. In my view, this compliance accounts for the fact that sociological models of stigma formation (i.e., labeling theory) were not supported by the evidence described herein—at least among the specialty POs interviewed for this investigation. While the evidence presented herein does not corroborate the formation of individual stigma among POs toward PMIs, this is not to say that PMIs are exempt from wider social stigma—but that question awaits further research in a future study.

Social Dominance, Institutionalized and Structural Stigma

This study also considered motivational models of stigma formation—and in particular, the authoritarian and social dominance theories, both of which are highly relevant in interpreting the data presented in Chapter 4. The probationary practices essentially functioned as well as they did because of the relative inequality between POs and PMIs. The former expected the compliance of the latter and used their authority and influence to implement and monitor probationary-mandated requirements. Despite the fact that unequal status is strongly correlated with stigma formation, there was no specific evidence of individual stigma toward the PMIs from POs—which is not to say that institutionalized stigma was not evident. The very structure of the probationary system transforms the offender from a human being interested in self-actualization into a second- class citizen. It could be argued that these men broke the law and deserve to be corralled into abiding by the letter of the law in whatever ways the court deems appropriate to protect the public's interests. However, stigma is present structurally because the rehabilitation and treatment process robs these individuals of their efficacy, decision-making capabilities, independence, and worth as human beings. Shoham & Rahav (1982) succinctly described the influence of larger institutional and structural mandates on less powerful and often marginalized offenders:

> The formal [more institutional form of] stigma imprinted or tagged on a person with a physical conspicuity signifying pollution are the Mark of Cain type of stigma, branded on criminals and sinners ... The common denominator seems to be the derogatory nature of the offences so that the branding tends to perpetuate and formalize the pollution and turpitude of their perpetrators.
>
> (Shoham & Rahav, 1982, p. 114)

This quote is interesting because of the power of this branding and signifying process. The work that POs do is diligent and sustained, often in challenging interpersonal situations with PMIs. However, in exercising processes of social and legal control, the PO is still exerting power and influence, while at the same time subduing pushback, because mandates are enforced in a humanistic manner. Some distinctions must be made between institutional and structural stigmas in order to ascertain their relative intentional or unintentional processes. Corrigan, Markowitz, and Watson (2004) summarized the difference:

> Mental illness strikes with a two-edged sword. On one side, people must struggle with the symptoms and disabilities that prevent them from achieving many of their life goals. On the other, the stigma of mental illness further hampers their opportunities and aspirations.
>
> (p. 489)

Structural models of stigma provides more understanding of the forms of prejudice and discrimination found within institutions that reflects socioeconomic, historical, and political forces. These forces that impact structural stigma could be intentional or unintentional, and reflect contemporary social structures reinvigorated by past forces of institutional discrimination. Historic forces related to mental health care still impact the ways that deviance and mental illness are addressed in the criminal justice system—and these practices have a tendency to impact stigma as well. The "throw them away and lock them up" ideology still influences how deviant behaviors (i.e., certain mental illnesses and crimes) are handled. These larger historical practices also impact political considerations that find their way into evolving mandates of the criminal justice system. The key element of structural stigma is not the intent but rather the effect of keeping certain groups in a subordinate position.

Revisiting Symbolic Interactionism and Grounded Theory

Symbolic interactionism (Blumer, 1969) provided another theoretical lens for evaluating interview data and capturing the sociological particularities of the PO–PMI probationary interactions. Three basic premises of this theory are germane to this investigation:

1   Individuals act toward things on the basis of the significances they attribute to those things.
2   The importance of such things is resultant from, or arises out of, the social interaction and engagement that the individual has with significant others and with the larger sociocultural context.
3   These significances are managed within, and adapted through, an explanatory manner used by the individual to deal with the things he encounters (Blumer, 1969).

In reference to the first premise, the PMIs engaged in their probationary mandates because each one agreed that these activities were important and needed for their current trajectories as rehabilitating offenders. Additionally, failing to engage resulted in highly undesirable consequences—which of course implies that significant behavioral conditioning was occurring. The fact that all six were fairly confident in a positive outcome at the end of their sentences indicated that the conditioning was working as intended and that they valued the experience as a means to an end—although acknowledged to be difficult at times.

The second premise—the importance of social interactions—was actualized during the PO–PMI dyads when I had the opportunity to observe their discussions, affirmations, questioning exchanges, and planning sessions. Clearly, the importance of every step of the probationary journey was reinforced and made more impactful through the social exchanges that occurred weekly or biweekly. The evidence shows that both parties used relational and interpersonal skills to accomplish two principal goals: (1) paint the best picture of the importance of following the rules (PO-directed), and (2) remain engaged enough to adhere to the expectations and mandates (PMI-directed). With respect to the former, POs used their social work skills and competencies to condition, validate, and affirm, or to chastise/punish the PMI for failing to conform or reach an agreed-upon goal. And the perceptions of POs as ally, mentor, and supportive system encouraged the PMI to admit failures and seek help.

The third premise of symbolic interactionism describes the process through which significances are managed within, and adapted through, an explanatory manner and how the individuals deal and cope with what they encounter. The explanatory process means that PMIs valued their freedom to such an extent that they were willing to relinquish their capacity for self-actualization and self-led decision-making in the hope that they could gain these back once they completed their probationary mandates. In swallowing their "bitter pill," they had also learned that making it go down a little easier meant learning to manage the requirements of probation by being a good and compliant probationer: listening to their PO, engaging openly and honestly, downplaying the constraints of probation, and taking care of business (i.e., adhering to their treatment mandates, attending to their reporting appointments, and participating in their rehabilitation of drug and alcohol and mental health needs).

The use of grounded theory viewed through the lens of the symbolic interactionism model assisted in conceptualizing the PMIs' probationary experiences. While these exchanges are embedded within a larger discourse about the efficacy of the criminal justice system as a whole, they elucidate the various social and psychological processes at work in how a specific and important subpopulation of the system is able to benefit from probationary mandates if they put in the effort and commit to long-lasting changes.

This grounded theory that probation is a type of behavioral and attitudinal training as a conduit to renewal and rehabilitation for PMIs is particularly interesting when compliance and adherence to mandates are examined from the multiple lens that this study facilitated. Compliance can mean different things at different milestones. In a criminal justice setting such as this one, adhering to mandates (or the reverse) has huge implications for the PMIs—eventual release from the system in presumably better psychosocial and physical health, or subjected to more restrictive sanctions, or worse. The PMIs in this study appear to have been conditioned and trained to understand the potential consequences of non-compliance. They have been equally trained to see the potential values related to following the requirements of the system. While admitting that it is ultimately impossible to understand each individual's true intrinsic and extrinsic motivations for adhering to mandates, these six men appeared to speak with one voice in describing the inherent benefits of their rehabilitation and treatment protocols.

Grounded theory aided in evaluating these social exchanges and assigning meaning as to how they perceived their individual experiences. The types of interpretations and meanings provided and the narratives of experiences from these participants provides a new understanding of the types of phenomenon being studied (i.e., interpersonal experiences, stigma, deviance, and perceptions of experiences in the criminal justice system). Symbolic interactionism can also be useful during this inductive and deductive process in that it helped provide a new and contextualized understanding of the setting, the people, and the interpersonal activities.

Contextualized Probation System: Some Additional Insights

Specialty probation afforded the PMIs who took part in this study a variety of targeted opportunities through treatment, rehabilitation, and self-help programs. In identifying and attempting to address complex issues of addiction, mental illness, and deviant behaviors that have ravaged their lives, they were trying to embark on a new life—and they appeared highly motivated to do so. Probationers routinely attended PO–PMI appointments and treatment appointments with their mental health and substance abuse counselors, as well as with other specialized providers. Although bound by court-mandated requirements, PMIs talked about their intrinsic motivations to succeed based on the perceived benefits of staying healthy through a variety of strategies. The evidence shows that PMIs' efforts were positively reinforced through more relational interpersonal exchanges with their POs. Those who were in compliance (i.e., in terms of attendance, mental-health treatment adherence, and focusing/working on abstinence from substances use) were motivated to get off probation in the quickest and most stress-free way possible. The narratives showed that PMIs valued these interpersonal exchanges, which created opportunities for mentorship and relationship building in their individual PO–PMI dyads. However, it must be noted that these PMIs could also have learned and been socialized to adhere to these mandates in order to gain certain privileges (i.e., better relationships with their POs, more leniency in expectations like being able to travel out of the county, etc.), and avoid further restrictive sanctions or jail time.

These probationers purposefully chose to comply for reasons individualized to their particular experience, or contextualized to the nature of criminal justice work. And working diligently for them from both a professional and humanistic perspective was a well-educated/trained specialty probation officer who appeared to genuinely want to impact the lives of their probationers towards better health and wellbeing. I observed both an objective and subjective use of power, judgment, hierarchical influence, skills, and tools to make these above-stated rehabilitation goals possible for these PMIs. The metaphor of "doing whatever it takes to get the job done" was evident in the PO narratives, in their observed professional interactions with their clients, and in their commitment to advanced training opportunities. In particular, the POs in the state where this study took place were afforded opportunities to be trained in the most up-to-date best practices needed to effectively work with both general probationers and PMIs. One such training opportunity, Motivational Interviewing, was heavily utilized by POs. It is

a counseling style that can be used with resistive offenders to move them forward towards positive change. It is about getting an offender to explore his or her problems in order to resolve ambivalence and move to acquire the knowledge, skills, and resources necessary to end criminal [and other problematic psychosocial] behavior[s].

(Abadinsky, 2012, p. 173)

Training opportunities such as MI are designed to enhance the skills and knowledge of probation officers so that they are better equipped to facilitate enduring, positive changes in the lives of individual probationers. This type of training is particularly suited for POs to work more on the counseling end of the treatment continuum described in Chapter 4 (i.e., using more therapeutic approaches and less criminal justice-oriented skills and tools to effect change in PMIs). The vision for using best practices and more therapeutic interventions is very explicit in the online criminal justice information database about probation work in this particular northeastern state. The vision for probation officers is focused on identifying and using evidence-based practices while making sure that probation officers possess the tools and resources to utilize the most effective interventions needed for effective identification, intervention of problems, and to reduce the recidivism rates of probationers.

These best practices are informed by general competencies in case management and various types of needs assessments of PMI challenges. Guiding their efforts is the desire to promote public safety, while at the same time trying to avoid the use of incarceration. For example, spurred by advances in technology, the toolkits of POs now include enhanced computer-aided technical assistance for the collection and dissemination of information between criminal justice professionals and agencies. Other specific "best practices interventions" include facilitating mental health services, job readiness and employment services referrals, and housing assistance. Also promoted are specific best practices related to working with probation-sentenced sex offenders, DWI offenders, and repeat drug-use offenders.

It is significant that there is a huge focus on providing alternatives to incarceration—and for multiple reasons. First, it usually costs more to incarcerate offenders at the local, state, and national levels than to offer community-based programs and rehabilitation services. Second, the needs of offenders are usually better served in the community as opposed to through more institutional means. Thus, keeping PMIs in compliance through community-based treatment options is a win–win for both the system and for the probationer—provided that public safety can be ensured. Moreover, with some exceptions, remaining in the community has more benefits, in that PMIs have access to family, friends, opportunities for psychosocial development, and the potential for safe and secure living arrangements. As summarized by PMI-B: "it all boils down to you stay good, they treat you good, and at the end of the day, they want to see you succeed. They want to see you not go back to jail."

Implications and Recommendations

Although the findings from this investigation emerged from narratives and observations of POs and PMIs situated in a single county criminal justice system in the northeast, this study is expected to inform the fields of criminal justice, sociology, psychology and counseling in other settings. In particular, however, the results detailed herein have particular relevance for (a) probation officers and other professional helpers (i.e., mental health and drug court professionals and parole officers) in the larger criminal justice system, (b) probation supervisors, and (c) professional counselor training programs.

Implications and Recommendations for PMIs and POs

To be successful in the rehabilitation, PMIs must be empowered to achieve and continue to strive for optimal health and behavioral changes that bolster their developmental capacities to grow and make pro-social decisions. As this investigation revealed, POs can and do play a significant role in helping PMIs achieve those goals through their ongoing personal support, accountability mandates, and behavioral expectations. The findings are revealing in that they elucidate the specific types of professional roles in which specialty probation officers engage PMIs on a regular basis as part of their work to manage rehabilitation services.

These results reinforce the need to offer more opportunities for POs to collaborate and engage with other professionals. As the findings show, POs valued the interagency resources and collaborative relationships that they have with other professionals and providers tasked with helping PMIs. These professional collaborations and active relationships are important for POs for both rehabilitation and treatment effectiveness, as well as to ensure that they are benefitting from the knowledge-based success of colleagues and other professionals.

As the evidence confirmed, the work of POs with PMIs is an arduous and challenging everyday responsibility from which POs cannot disengage—especially since their primary responsibility is to maintain public safety. Because the work of helping PMIs prevent relapses and recidivist behaviors is often demanding and strenuous, it will be important for probation officers to engage in continuous self-care and reinvigorating experiences that promote their own mental and physical health and wellbeing. A psychologically, physically, and interpersonally healthy probation officer will be able to provide better care and support across a range of different presenting problems in comparison to a burned-out professional.

In addition to addressing their own wellbeing in ways that will enrich their personal and professional lives, POs must also have to use introspection and self-awareness as professional tools to work under challenging circumstances, with often difficult client systems and issues. POs must understand the challenging and often unexamined stigmas that impact the lives and wellbeing of their probationers. As such, they must be open and available to engage in current professional knowledge and educational opportunities that will provide this exposure and expertise as part of their available toolkits. Stigma is often an unexamined aspect of one's life and experience until a challenge or exposure to aversive situations becomes a reality. It is important for POs to constantly examine and re-examine their work and capacities and learn to assimilate the needed best practices to work in a non-stigmatizing way. Accountability is a major element for professionals in service professions that cater to the public, and probation officers are and should be held accountable, particularly because of the high profile nature of their work and service to the community. The many opportunities that POs have to engage in professional development should include the proven and effective stigma-mitigating processes that will benefit them in their roles and work with offenders with co-occurring mental health and psychosocial needs. Ongoing training opportunities, awareness and insight, and hands-on supervisory practices represent important considerations to make this re-examination possible.

Implications for Probation Supervisors

Probation supervisors should be equipped with knowledge from current professional development opportunities that will support and bolster the practices of their supervisees. The importance of PO specialty training in increasing knowledge and skills was a persistent theme that emerged from this investigation. Hence, the significance of skilled supervisory support in ensuring that PMIs are receiving the best care and oversight possible from their POs cannot be overstated. While it must be noted that administrative oversight and supervision of POs work was not a focus of this study, probation supervisors must feel empowered to support their POs in ways that facilitate positive professional behaviors, accountability, and practice. In particular, such oversight will help to ensure the use of non-stigmatizing methods that do not reinforce the stereotypes concerning probation officers and criminal justice professionals.

As this investigation revealed, there are some important differences between traditional probation officers and specialty officers with respect to the clientele they serve. These differences directly impact the knowledge that POs possess and the probationary practices they employ. Therefore, supervisors must be aware of the specialized needs of PMIs and the specific personal and professional attributes that a PO should possess in order to serve as allies, mentors, and supporters. In addition, administrators and supervisors ultimately hold the power as to how programs are structured and maintained. These individuals should strive to design effective probation programs and services and ensure that power differentials between the officer and the probationer are monitored. The staff should be equipped with the most effective tools to ensure treatment adherence in ways that do not dehumanize the life and personhood of the PMI.

Implications for Professional Counseling Training Programs

As the evidence shows, a growing number of probation officers are working toward and attaining undergraduate and postgraduate training at the bachelor's and master's level in mental health counseling and substance abuse counseling in preparation for their work as professional specialty POs. As such, it is important for university-based and professional training programs to consider implementing educational opportunities for those interested in working in the criminal justice system. Degree programs and/or seminars could be enhanced with opportunities to gain real-life professional experiences as practicum and internship students. Counselor-educators and professional licensed counselors could become effective mentors and supervisors for these students.

Additionally, trainees will ultimately benefit if they are matched with local mentors who have and continue to make use of their identities as mental health counselors, substance abuse interventionists, and criminal justice professionals.

Potential Limitations of the Study

One of the potential limitations of this study has to do with the operationalization of mental illness as a construct. Indeed, this was an issue in developing this study due to lack of agreement as to (a) what mental illness is, (b) the relative differences between the nature and presentation of mental illness as an experience cross-culturally and cross-contextually, (c) how it should be measured, and (d) how it impacts the rehabilitative and treatment experience of probationers. The complexity of these factors may have impacted the type of data that was collected from PMIs. To address this potential limitation, I used discrete DSM-IV-TR criteria (i.e., by having the PMIs self-identify their specific diagnoses) as a unifying template to ensure some agreement as to the nature of the problems for which PMIs were receiving treatment and rehabilitation services. The PMIs selected for participation in this study all met criteria for DSM-IV-TR diagnoses and were active in mental health and/or substance abuse counseling as a part of their rehabilitation and treatment sentences at the time of data collection. In addition, these criteria were used to identify PMIs that would be hindered, challenged, or hurt psychologically by participating in the study. Probationers with psychotic or thought disorders were excluded from participating in this study.

This study features a methodological limitation in terms of its design and the data-collection strategies employed herein. The goal in qualitative studies is to ensure that the data being collected is representative and also contains rich contextual information. The data-collection processes in this investigation were limited in that individual interviews and participant observations were the sole means of collecting data. Although some data saturation was possible by the end of the data-collection timeline, the limited timeframe used in gathering data in this research and the condensed data-collection strategies represent potential drawbacks in reaching data saturation. Additionally, the data-collection context for this study is unique to a single county criminal justice setting in a northeast state. While I believe the findings described herein are representative of what is taking place around the country in terms of specialty probation settings with POs and PMIs, the results from this investigation cannot be generalized to all criminal justice settings. There are potential limitations of transferability of the findings in this localized contexts to other probation settings, which include a variety of constructs (i.e., regional cultural differences, regional differences in beliefs and practices, different administrative practices, and varied types of hierarchies and flow of responsibilities, etc.). These and other considerations could potentially impact how relevant these findings will be when compared to similarly designed county probation settings in other parts of the country as the one described in this research.

Another limitation that must be noted pertains to full disclosure—i.e., the possibility that probationers may have felt threatened or fearful of discussing their personal histories or the specifics of their probation requirements. As noted earlier, there was overwhelming positivity in how the PMIs described the personal and professional dispositions of their individual POs. Nonetheless, it is possible that the threat of sanctions could have played a role in types of narratives that PMIs shared relative to their experiences with their probation officers. Similarly, POs could have felt compelled to answer interview questions in a socially desirable way because of a fear of putting their jobs in jeopardy. To reduce this likelihood, I made sure to inform the participants during the informed consent process that the confidentiality of participants' disclosures would be maintained throughout the course of the data-collection process and in the analysis and reporting of the findings.

In addition, there are benefits involved in conducting this study with young adult males between the ages of 20 and 30 years old. It is possible that a different age cohort, or one including females, could have produced different findings. Thus, this study's results are ultimately only potentially generalizable to young adult male PMIs. As such, subsequent studies could benefit from the voices and experiences of different individuals and cohorts as a way of expanding knowledge of this important topic.

There are also limitations in the processes used to select the PMI-subjects. Selection bias is a potentially difficult and challenging issue to resolve in qualitative research. Given the sensitive nature of this topic, identifying and choosing PMIs who fit certain criteria (i.e., compliant with attending appointments and not disruptive or severely mentally ill) represents a form of selection bias. As such, this limitation has the potential to influence the types of data collected from subjects. It is possible that the process used to identify, recruit, and select the six PMIs who took part in this study inadvertently omitted others whose narratives would have provided different perspectives. Although generalization of the findings is not a major concern in qualitative research, there are trade-offs that were made in the sense that data obtained from these six men represents a largely unified perspective—although a rich and detailed one. It is possible that having a more comprehensive subject selection process could have produced a variety of other findings as to the nature of the PMI probation experience. Indeed, in recommending an alternate approach, hearing about the narratives of "other" types of probationers, such as those who were not compliant and routinely violated the terms of their probation sentences, would certainly be both interesting and worthwhile. However, monetary and temporal resources were limited for conducting an expanded investigation at the time this study was initiated.

Recommendations for Future Research

The design and purpose of this qualitative investigation were informed by (a) the interdisciplinary nature of the researcher's interests, and (b) the desire to make a scholarly contribution to the fields of Criminal Justice, Mental Health and Addictions Counseling, Sociology, and Social Psychology. This study was designed to obtain a multifaceted and multi-perspectival view of what it means to be on probation—primarily via the lens of probationers with mental illness, but secondarily from the viewpoint of the probation officers who supervise them. More qualitative research is needed with more diverse samples of probationers to offer comparative findings across a variety of demographics.

For example, further empirical work is needed to compare the experiences of minority probationers with other majority groups in the probation system (i.e., comparing the experiences of probationers of African descent with those of European origin or other groups), as well as to assess the effects of minority group membership, ethnicity, and race on perceived or experienced stigma. As noted above, other studies should be undertaken that include women probationers and PMIs of different ages.

Additionally, a more comprehensive study should be undertaken to examine PMIs' rehabilitation experiences in the larger community outside of the confines of the probation office. Such a study could be achieved by engaging the PMIs in settings external to the county probation setting—such as with their mental health counselors or in group settings that address problems of addiction. These varied settings could add significant insights into the challenging and diverse contextual issues they face. Although potentially both costly and risky for a researcher to embed him or herself in a community setting where they (and potentially more dangerous individuals) spend their time, it would nonetheless add to our understanding of the challenges of living with the realities of deviance, mental illness, and addictions—not to mention how stigma plays a role in perpetuating this multi-tiered problem.

References

Abadinsky, H. (2012). *Probation and parole. Theory and practice*. Upper Saddle River, NJ: Pearson Education, Inc.

Allen, G. F. (1985). The probationers speak: Analysis of the probationers' experiences and attitudes. *Federal Probation*, 49, 67–75.

Beckett, K., & Sasson, T. (2000). The war on crime as hegemonic strategy: A neo-Marxian theory of the new punitiveness in US criminal justice policy. In S. S. Simpson (Ed.), *Of Crime and Criminality*, (pp. 61–85). Thousand Oaks, CA: Pine Forge Press.

Blumer, H. (1969). *Symbolic interactionism: Perspective and method*. Englewood Cliffs, NJ: Prentice Hall.

Byrne, P. (2000). Stigma of mental illness and ways of diminishing it. *Advances in Psychiatric Treatment*, 6, 65–72.

Corrigan, P. W., Markowitz, F. E., & Watson, A. C. (2004). Structural levels of mental illness stigma and discrimination. *Schizophrenia Bulletin*, 30(3), 481–491.

DeLude, B., Mitchell, D., & Barber, C. (2012). The probationer's perspective on the probation officer-probationer relationship and satisfaction with probation. *Federal Probation*, 76, 35–48.

Dmitrieva, J., Monahan, K. C., Cauffman, E., & Steinberg, L. (2012). Arrested development: The effects of incarceration on the development of psychosocial maturity. *Development and Psychopathology*, 24, 1073–1090.

Erikson, E. H. (1968). *Identity: Youth and crisis*. New York, NY: Norton.

Giordano, P. C., Cernkovich, S. A., & Rudolph, J. L. (2002). Gender, crime, and desistance: Toward a theory of cognitive transformation. *American Journal of Sociology*, 107(4), 990–1064.

Goffman, E. (1963). *Stigma: Notes on the management of spoiled identity*. New York, NY: Simon & Schuster, Inc.

Hartwell, S. (2004). Triple stigma: Persons with mental illness and substance abuse problems in the criminal justice system. *Criminal Justice Policy Review*, 15(1), 84–99.

Healy, D., & O'Donnell, I. (2008). Calling time on crime: Motivation, generativity and agency in Irish probationers. *The Journal of Community and Criminal Justice*, 55(1), 25–38.

Kras, K. R. (2013). Offender perceptions of mandated substance abuse treatment: An exploratory analysis of offender experiences in a community-based treatment program. *Journal of Drug Issues*, 43(2), 124–143.

Maggs, J. L., Frome, P. M., Eccles, J. S., & Barber, B. L. (1997). Psychosocial resources, adolescent risk behavior and young adult adjustment: is risk taking more dangerous for some than others? *Journal of Adolescence*, 20, 103–119.

Miller, P. H. (2002). *Theories of developmental psychology*. New York, NY: Worth Publishers.

Munley, P. H. (1977). Erikson's theory of psychosocial development and career development. *Journal of Vocational Behavior*, 10, 261–269.

Shoham, S. G., & Rahav, G. (1982). *The Mark of Cain: The stigma theory of crime and social deviance*. New York, NY: St. Martin's Press.

Skeem, J. L., & Louden, J. E. (2006). Toward evidence-based practice for probationers and parolees mandated to mental health treatment. *Psychiatric Services*, 57(3), 333–342.

Appendix A
PMI Questionnaire

First Round of Interviews (Day 1)

1 How long have you been on probation and what was the reason for your probation sentence?
2 What are some of your requirements for probation? How do you meet these requirements? For example, looking for work, mental health and substance abuse counseling, school and education?
3 How does your reporting requirement(s) affect your [daily, weekly and/or monthly schedule] routine?
4 Describe your probation sentence? What are some of the highs and lows?
5 Do you experience any problems with POs or any other person related to you having a mental health issue?
6 What kinds of stress, anxiety, and depression do you experience and how do these issues impact your life?
7 How would you describe how you are affected by the requirements of your probation sentence? What are your impressions of the expectations/what your PO expects and of the daily, weekly, and/or monthly reporting requirements that you have to do?
8 How would you describe your interaction and relationship with your probation officer?
9 What thing(s) about probation sentence negatively impacts you?

Second Round of Interviews (Day 2)

1 How would you describe the ways that you are treated as probationer by your PO and by probation as a whole?
2 Do you perceive anything negative about the way that your PO and/or probation as whole treat you as a person? If so, please describe.
3 What are some of the good things that you get from your interaction with your probation officer? What are some of the not so good things in this interaction?

4   How would you describe your experience in probation as a whole? What are some of things that have impacted your probation sentence, good and bad?

5   If you could change some things about your probation sentence and experience, what would you change? And why would you want these changes?

6   If you could change some things about the ways your probation officer interacts with you and how he or she works with you, what would you change? And why would you want these changes?

7   What impacts and/or affects your probation sentence and experience?

8   How do you cope/deal with being on probation? What kinds of things do you do to make probation easier to adjust to and live with?

9   Do you have any other information that you can share about your probation that will help me get a better perspective of your probation experience?

Appendix B
PO Questionnaire

First Round of Interviews (Day 1)

1 How would you describe your work as a probation officer?
2 How would you describe the tools and expertise that you use with your probationers?
3 How do you use these tools and expertise?
4 What is your level of educational attainment (i.e., bachelor's and/or master's)?
5 What was your area of concentration in school (i.e., counseling, social work, criminal justice, sociology, psychology, other)?
6 How did your education and training prepare you for this work?
7 What factors impact your work as a probation officer? And how do these factors impact your practice as a probation officer?
8 What is your perception about mental illness?
9 Have you had dealings and experiences with individuals with mental illness in your private, personal life and professional life?
10 Do these interactions/dealings impact the way you see people with mental illness?

Second Round of Interviews (Day 2)

1 How would you describe your relationship and interactions with your probationers?
2 What are some of the practices that you engage in as a probation officer in working with probationers? In other words how do you practice probation services?
3 What are some of the institutional/systemic mandates that influence your daily work as a probation officer?

4 If there are ambiguities, how do you work to resolve the ambiguities between practice mandates and working to rehabilitate and/or provide care to your probationers?

5 What kinds of needs do your probationers have and how do you work to help them resolve these needs?

6 What are some of the successes and challenges that you have experienced in your position as a PO and in your work with PMIs?

7 What kinds of training and professional development/continuing education do you engage in as a probation officer? How often do you engage in professional development?

8 What kinds of impact do these training opportunities offer you as a criminal justice service professional?

Is there any other information that you can share with me that will give me a better perspective into how you provide probation service and on how you engage your probationers?

Appendix C
Specialty Probation Departments

The specialty probation departments within this local probation and county community correction specialized service include:

1 **A DWI unit** that supervises probationers who are primarily multiple drinking-driver offenders. The unit coordinates the office's DWI surveillance program by observing high-risk DWI offenders. Referral to specialized chemical dependency/DWI treatments in the community is also a part of this department's responsibility.

2 **The Domestic Violence Intervention unit** is another department within the larger probation system in this county. This unit provides adult, family services, and conducts intake services to assist victims of domestic violence by preparing family court orders of protection and by referring probationers to services in the community.

3 **The intensive supervision program** is another unit focused on the provision of specialized services in a variety of formats. This unit supervises high-risk probationers who have been diverted from the state division of correctional services. The unit provides an intensive modality of treatments services to probationers as well as an exhaustive frequency of case contacts at the office and at home. Individuals with mental health and substance abuse problems are referred to treatment in the community and interface with their probation officers on a regular basis.

Index